ETHICAL ASPECTS
OF
HEALTH CARE
FOR THE
ELDERLY

ETHICAL ASPECTS
OF
HEALTH CARE
FOR THE
ELDERLY

An Annotated Bibliography

COMPILED BY
MARSHALL B. KAPP

Bibliographies and Indexes in Gerontology, Number 17
Erdman B. Palmore, Series Adviser

Greenwood Press
Westport, Connecticut • London

Library of Congress Cataloging-in-Publication Data

Kapp, Marshall B.
    Ethical aspects of health care for the elderly : an annotated
bibliography / compiled by Marshall B. Kapp.
        p.   cm.—(Bibliographies and indexes in gerontology, ISSN
0743-7560 ; no. 17)
    ISBN 0-313-27490-8 (alk. paper)
    1. Aged—Medical care—Moral and ethical aspects—Bibliography.
I. Series.
Z6673.35.K36   1992 RC952
[.5]
016.174'2—dc20   92-17776

British Library Cataloguing in Publication Data is available.

Library of Congress Catalog Card Number: 92-17776
ISBN: 0-313-27490-8
ISSN: 0743-7560

First published in 1992

Greenwood Press, 88 Post Road West, Westport, CT 06881
An imprint of Greenwood Publishing Group, Inc.

Printed in the United States of America

The paper used in this book complies with the
Permanent Paper Standard issued by the National
Information Standards Organization (Z39.48-1984).

10 9 8 7 6 5 4 3 2 1

Contents

Foreword

The annotated bibliographies in this series provide answers to the fundamental question, "What is known?" Their purpose is simple, yet profound: to provide comprehensive reviews and references for the work done in various fields of gerontology. They are based on the fact that it is no longer possible for anyone to comprehend the vast body of research and writing in even one sub-specialty without years of work.

This fact has become true only in recent years. When I was an undergraduate (Class of '52) I think no one at Duke had even heard of gerontology. Almost no one in the world was identified as a gerontologist. Now there are over 6,000 professional members of the Gerontological Society of America. When I was an undergraduate there was only one gerontological journal (the Journal of Gerontology, begun in 1945). Now there are over forty professional journals and several dozen books in gerontology published each year.

The reasons for this dramatic growth are well known: the dramatic increase in numbers of the aged, the shift from family to public responsibility for the security and care of the elderly, the recognition of aging as a "social problem," and the growth of science in general. It is less well known that this explosive growth in knowledge has developed the need for new solutions to the old problem of comprehending and "keeping up" with a field of knowledge. The old indexes and library card catalogues have become increasingly inadequate for the job. On-line computer indexes and abstracts are one solution but make no evaluation selections nor organize sources logically as is done here. These annotated bibliographies are also more widely available than on-line computer indexes.

These bibliographies will obviously be useful for students and researchers who need to know what research has (or has not) been done in their field. The annotations contain enough information so that the researcher usually does not have to search out the original articles. In the past, the "review of literature" has often been haphazard and was rarely comprehensive, because of the large investment of time (and money) that would be required by a truly comprehensive review. Now, using these bibliographies, researchers can be more confident that they are not missing important previous research; they can be more confident that they are not duplicating past efforts and "reinventing the wheel." It may well become standard and expected practice for researchers to consult such bibliographies, even before they start their research.

Ethical aspects of health care is one of the fastest growing topics in gerontology and geriatrics. One of the main reasons is the escalating costs of health care. These costs are being pushed up by more sophisticated technology, more procedures available, more elders needing health care, rising expectations about needs for health care, and lack of effective cost controls in our health care system.

All these factors have ethical implications and create ethical dilemmas. There is a general fear that unless something is done, these costs will bankrupt Medicare and lead to a general breakdown of our health care system. The rapid growth in concern about ethical aspects of health care has led to a rapid growth in research and writing about the field. Thus, a comprehensive bibliography in this area is one of the most useful and important in gerontology.

This book is needed not only by academics, researchers, and students, but also by health professionals and others who work with elders, as well as by elders themselves, their families, and anyone else interested in health care.

The author has done an outstanding job of covering all the recent literature and organizing it into easily accessible form. Not only are there 533 annotated references organized into 11 chapters, there are also an introduction, a preface, an author index, and a subject index with many cross-references for the items in the bibliography.

Thus, one can look for relevant material in this volume in several ways: (1) look up a given subject in the subject index; (2) look up a given author in the author index; or (3) turn to the section that covers the topic.

The author, Marshall B. Kapp, J.D., M.P.H., is exceptionally well qualified to prepare this bibliography. He is Professor of Community Health and Director of the Office of Geriatric Medicine and Gerontology at Wright State University, Dayton, OH. He has done research and produced 21 publications relevant to this field. One of these publications is a related bibliography in this series, <u>Legal Aspects of Health Care for the Elderly</u>. His annotations are clear and concise so that they are easy to read and understand.

So it is with great pleasure that we add this bibliography to our series. We believe you will find this volume to be the most useful, comprehensive, and easily accessible reference work in its field. I will appreciate any comments you care to send me.

Erdman B. Palmore
Center for the Study of Aging and Human Development
Box 3003, Duke University Medical Center
Durham, NC 27710

Preface

The entries in this volume consist of references to articles, books, reports, and organizational policy statements. They are organized by chapter according to primary ethical topic. I have endeavored to separate these topics broadly enough to be manageable, but precisely enough to be descriptive. Since many entries span a variety of ethical topics, the organization is supplemented by cross-referencing through the index. There are separate author and subject indexes, with index numbers correlating to entry numbers rather than pages.

The collection of sources contained in this annotated bibliography is selective, rather than pretending to approach comprehensiveness. Several specific selection criteria were purposely utilized.

First, all references included here were published originally between January 1, 1980 and October 1, 1991. The latter cutoff date was chosen for purposes of manageability. The beginning date represents the judgment that, while many significant and pertinent discussions of ethical aspects of health care for the elderly appeared prior to the last decade, most are much more recent. Given the pace of relevant scientific, financial, social, and legal developments in the area of geriatric care and the maturation and multiplication of corresponding professional literature inspired by the ethical implications of those developments, the material included in this volume is as up-to-date as possible.

Second, references are listed here only if they deal explicitly with an "ethical" aspect of health care for the elderly, as opposed to the numerous other aspects that might be discussed. Some of the sources cited here deal primarily with one of these other aspects, but consciously mention important ethical concerns. For inclusion in this volume, an aspect of health care for the elderly is considered "ethical" in nature if it is so characterized by the author of the piece or if, in this compiler's judgment, it would be chiefly characterized as such by a health care provider, a philosopher, an older health care consumer or family member, or an attorney.

This author made the decision to exclude from this listing a number of valuable books and articles that deal exclusively or almost so with the legal dimensions of health care for the elderly (see my earlier Annotated Bibliography). Certainly, ethical and legal aspects frequently are inextricably intertwined, and ethical positions concerning health care problems often cannot be comprehended adequately without a thorough acquaintance with relevant legal requirements that color the ethical landscape. Many of the sources cited here provide extensive and eloquent expositions about that legal environment. However, ethics and law are not synonymous. Unless a book or journal article devote some noticeable attention to specific, identified ethical issues and principles, that source was not included.

Third, references are included here only if they deal with the older health care consumer. This means that sources discussing only generic medical ethics concepts, with no particular attention to the elderly, tended to be excluded. If, though, a generic medical ethics discussion could reasonably be read to have specific bearing on the special needs and characteristics of the older patient, that discussion was a candidate for selection. Additionally, sources examining only ethical concerns of the elderly outside of the health care setting, such as involving income maintenance programs, did not enter this volume. The clear emphasis here is on health care issues, although that domain has been interpreted quite broadly.

Finally, potential sources were disqualified from inclusion here if, in this compiler's opinion, they were either so patently inaccurate or poorly written that they would not be helpful to the reader. Use of this criterion in no way warrants that selected sources therefore are uniformly accurate or well-written. Conversely, many excellent sources were omitted under other selection criteria or (more likely) due to the compiler's oversight.

The references that were selected for inclusion here are taken from prominent medical, nursing, ethics, health administration, and (to a much lesser extent) legal literature. Major textbooks in geriatric medicine were examined, as were card catalogues. Among the journals that the author manually researched were post 1980 editions of: <u>Hastings Center Report</u>; <u>Gerontologist</u>; <u>Generations</u>; <u>Journal of the American Geriatrics Society</u>; <u>Law, Medicine & Health Care</u>; <u>Annals of Internal Medicine</u>; <u>Archives of Internal Medicine</u>; <u>New England Journal of Medicine</u>; <u>Journal of the American Medical Association</u>; <u>Issues in Law and Medicine</u>; <u>American Journal of Law and Medicine</u>; and <u>Journal of Legal Medicine</u>.

The sources cited in this volume should be readily available through most college or university libraries and many good public libraries, particularly through interlibrary loan. Books may be obtained directly from their publishers and journals may be obtained from the organizations that publish them.

In preparing this volume, the able assistance of Dr. Erdman B. Palmore, series editor and Dr. George F. Butler, Acquisitions Editor for Social and Behavioral Sciences at Greenwood Press, is gratefully acknowledged. I also express my sincere appreciation for expert librarial assistance provided by the staffs of the Wright State University Health Sciences Library and the University of Dayton Law Library. Last but not least, I thank Ms. Christina DeWitt for her diligence and care in the processing of this manuscript.

<u>Ethical Aspects of Health Care for the Elderly: An Annotated Bibliography</u> is intended to be an educational tool. The end to which this volume is a means is the provision of health and human services in a manner that best respects the autonomy, dignity, and well-being of older individuals while promoting the ethical integrity of the service provider. The achievement of this goal ultimately will depend less on the tool itself than on how well the artisan--the reader--interprets and utilizes its contents.

Introduction

As noted in my 1988 Annotated Bibliography, <u>Legal Aspects of Health Care for the Elderly</u>, health care for older persons involves much more than an understanding of human biology. It involves a rich and complicated pattern of human relationships, encompassing the older person, the family, the physician, other members of the health care team, social service professionals, institutions and their administrators and trustees, private third-party payors and reviewers, government agencies, and the public. These relationships largely determine the access that older persons will enjoy to health care and the quality and affordability of services received. As explained in my earlier book, these relationships are guided heavily by rules--including legal requirements--that collectively we either explicitly announce or implicitly understand as necessary for the maintenance of a just and orderly society.

The relationships which shape health care for the elderly are also influenced powerfully by ethical considerations--moral principles that define acceptable substantive norms of conduct and fair procedures for applying those norms in particular fact patterns. The interplay of ethics and medicine has been recognized, at least implicitly, since ancient times. Ethical principles relating to informed consent, confidentiality, and abatement of medical treatment predate Hippocrates. Yet, as society in general and medical science in particular have grown steadily in complexity, sophistication, and expectations, ethical precepts have become increasingly entangled in the whole panoply of medical decisions and decision making. Today, the proper delivery of health and human services demands a familiarity with, and respect for, those ethical precepts.

Literature attempting to analyze, explain, and on occasion criticize the ethics/health care relationship generally has a long and distinguished history. The elderly comprise one particular subset of health care consumers. Most generic topics in medical ethics affect the elderly as well as potential patients of other ages. Conversely, most ethical issues faced by older patients also arise in the case of younger persons who adopt, or have thrust upon them, the patient role. However, even generic ethical questions more often than not take on unique twist and connotations when older patients are involved. Thus, a unique body of ethical theory concerned with personal and institutional relationships, implicated by the delivery of health care for the elderly, is evolving. Concomitantly, a separate literature devoted to explicating, discussing, and suggesting improvements in that theoretical corpus is slowly but surely developing.

Examples of literature describing and analyzing these ethical considerations--what is the right thing to do, and who should decide and according to what criteria and using what decisionmaking processes--form the content of the current volume. On many points, the intersection of ethics, aging, and health care lacks clarity and definitude. Principles and approaches for problem identification and resolution are taking firmer shape, though, and health care and human service professionals must be conversant with them. As these principles and analytic and procedural approaches evolve, so too does the literature explaining and contributing to their evolution. In the past decade, the literature has exploded to the point that some careful organization and direction is needed if the literature is to be useful. This annotated bibliography tries to make this literature less intimidating and more accessible to those who must understand and implement it for the benefit of the older health care consumer.

Chapter One contains a number of general sources on ethics, health care, aging, and advocacy. The reader can examine these sources first to obtain an overall background regarding the subject area before plunging into more specific material. The coverage of pieces included in this chapter is too broad to allow pigeonholing into one of the other chapters.

Chapter Two deals in essence with the ethical principle of autonomy, or self-determination: the right of the older person to make personal decisions and to "do his or her own thing" free of external interference or intervention. This encompasses such issues as mental capacity (a preferable term to competency) and informed consent. It additionally includes issues relating to the safeguarding and management of personal information about the older patient and to the therapeutic relationship between older patient and professional caregiver generally.

In the modern health care system, more and more financial concerns seem to determine and delimit options regarding the form and amount of care that the patient may have available. Chapter Three deals with the impact of economic factors on health care of older persons, including current proposals and counterproposals about utilization of chronological age as the criterion for allocating or rationing scarce health resources.

Chapter Four covers a variety of ethical issues that arise for older persons receiving services in institutional and community settings. The sources cited here frequently reflect the tension between the principle of beneficence or protection, which can sometimes devolve into paternalism, on one hand (as represented by guardianship and protective services), and the principle of autonomy, which can sometimes devolve into situations of abuse or neglect, on the other. The role of family caregiving and entry into and discharge from institutional care are explored here.

Sources falling under the popular rubric of "death with dignity" or "right to die" comprise Chapter Five. Suicide, assisted suicide, active and passive euthanasia, the right to refuse life-sustaining medical interventions, and decisionmaking for mentally incapacitated persons (including the severely demented, depressed, and persistently vegetative) are the central topics covered.

The role and limits of institutional ethics committees and formal ethics consultations are spelled out in Chapter Six. These devices are being implemented by many health care institutions to assist in resolving the kinds of dilemmas discussed in the previous chapter. Since one of the main forms of life-sustaining medical intervention generating ethical controversy is cardiopulmonary resuscitation, a substantial body of literature exploring the ethical implications of CPR decisions has developed. This body of literature is reflected in Chapter Seven.

As health care professionals are coming to accept the reasonable limits of medical science in treating critically ill patients, those professionals and their institutions are facing a growing number of situations where patients and/or their families are demanding forms of medical intervention that the professionals believe to be futile or even harmful. Chapter Eight revolves around the emerging subject of medical futility.

One way that older individuals, their families, and health care institutions and professionals can obviate or mitigate some of the dilemmas raised by the selections in the previous four chapters is by advance health care planning. The ethical connotations and efficacy of devices such as living wills, durable powers of attorney, and values histories are delved into in Chapter Nine.

Chapter Ten is concerned with issues in the definition of death and the treatment and potential beneficial uses of cadavers. The final chapter deals with the complicated question of participation by older persons, often institutionalized and/or suffering from severe cognitive deficits, as human subjects in biomedical and behavioral research aimed at problems plaguing the very population which lacks mental capacity to engage in the ordinary version of informed consent.

This volume is intended to assist practicing health and human service professionals, as well as researchers, teachers, and students in the health and human service fields in more easily identifying and locating relevant sources of information and guidance. Ethicists, clergy and other pastoral counselors, attorneys, philosophy and clergy students, and law students should also find this book useful. Hopefully, members of the general public, especially older individuals and their families, will find this volume valuable also.

ENTRIES BY TOPIC

1
General Sources on Ethics, Health Care, Aging, and Advocacy

1. Bernat, James L. Ethical and Legal Duties of the Contemporary Physician. Pharos; Spring 1989; 52(2): 29-32.

This paper outlines the major ethical and legal responsibilities of the practicing physician today. These include duties to the patient, the family, other physicians, and society. Many of the modern physician's obligations have special application to the care of older adults.

2. Caplan, Arthur L.; Callahan, Daniel; Haas, Janet. Ethical & Policy Issues in Rehabilitation Medicine. Hastings Center Report; August 1987; 17(4): 1-20 Supplement.

This report of a Hastings Center project analyzes ethical issues that arise in the context of providing rehabilitation medicine to the physically and mentally disabled. Ethical discussion revolves around such questions as the selection of patients (both initially and for particular courses of care), the appropriate model for the provider/patient relationship (paternalism vs. contractual vs. educational), termination of treatment, family duties and rights, team and interprofessional dynamics, and resource allocation.

3. Cassel, Christine K. Ethical Problems in Geriatric Medicine. in: Cassel, Christine K.; Riesenberg, Donald E.; Sorenson, Leif B.; Walsh, John R., Editors. Geriatric Medicine. Second ed. New York: Springer-Verlag; 1990: 38-47.

This is an overview of everyday ethical issues facing the geriatrician. It first explains the guiding principles of beneficence, respect for persons, fidelity or trust, and distributive justice as they apply to health care for the elderly. This chapter then discusses the ethical components of informed consent: information sharing, lack of coercion, and assessment of decisional capacity. Decisions to forego life-sustaining treatment are explored, with attention to the concepts of brain death, persistent vegetative state, quality of life, and artificial nutrition and hydration. Special ethical challenges in nursing homes are mentioned.

4. Cassel, Christine K.; Goldstein, Mary K. Ethical Considerations. in: Jarvik, Lissy F; Winograd, Carol H., Editors. Treatments for the Alzheimer Patient--The Long Haul. New York: Springer Publishing Company; 1988: 80-95.

The authors discuss fundamental principles of biomedical ethics (respect for persons, beneficence, justice), practical approaches to ethical dilemmas in medicine, the role of the health professional as ethicist, and particular ethical problems that arise in the care of Alzheimer's patients. Special attention is paid to medical decision making where the patient is not personally decisionally capable, including decisions to institutionalize an individual, and to equitable distribution of the costs of care. The role of the family is analyzed.

5. Cassell, Eric J. Recognizing Suffering. Hastings Center Report; May/June 1991; 21(3): 24-31.

Dr. Cassell ponders the moral meaning of human suffering. Learning about suffering is important to clinical ethics, he contends, because of the light it sheds on the nature of persons and individuality. Understanding in ethics grows not only through the evolution of theory but through the expansion of knowledge about the subject of ethics--persons. The author uses case studies involving older patients to illustrate key concepts.

6. Churchill, Larry R. Ethical Issues in Chronic, Severe, and Catastrophic Illnesses. Southern Medical Journal; July 1989; 82(7): 815-817.

Philosopher Churchill identifies the three major problems of the American health care system as escalating costs, limited access, and lack of consensus on the social purpose of medicine. He addresses each problem briefly and indicates how medical ethics is centrally implicated. The moral paradigms we have used to think about health care are ill-equipped to help us resolve our current chief problems, especially delineation of what the purposes of our health care system are to be. Dealing with chronic, severe, and catastrophic illnesses will require a new, robust ethic that looks at what should be done when it is impossible to do everything. The issue is not one of benevolence, but of justice and fairness.

7. Cohen, Elias S. Realism, Law & Aging. Law, Medicine & Health Care; Fall 1990; 18(3): 183-192.

This article examines the cultural context of old age in the United States and the ways in which the law, as an instrument of society's ethical values, is shaped by social attitudes toward the elderly and how the law, in turn, helps to shape social attitudes toward older persons. Cohen speculates about how changing demographic patterns will effect what it will mean to grow old in America in the future.

8. Cohen, Elias S. The Elderly Mystique: Impediment to Advocacy and Empowerment. Generations; 1990; 14(Supplement): 13-16.

This article addresses the special problems that attend efforts to empower elders who have disabilities and to advocate on their behalf. Cohen explores the notion that the language of geriatrics and gerontology reflects a deeply embedded and generally held belief, shared by elderly people themselves, that potentials for growth, development, and continuing engagement virtually disappear when an elderly person suffers a serious disability.

9. Cole, Thomas R. Aging and Meaning. Generations; Winter 1985; 10(2): 49-52.

Historian Cole examines contemporary cultural attitudes toward aging and the aged, and the ethical implications of those attitudes. He argues that older persons are consistently undervalued in a materialistic and youth-oriented culture.

10. Cole, Thomas R. The Enlightened View of Aging: Victorian Morality in a New Key. Hastings Center Report; June 1983; 13(3): 34-40.

This essay critically reviews cultural attitudes toward, and characterizations of, aging and the aged. In his search for the meaning of old age, Cole rejects both poles of dualism as mythology: the ageism which characterizes all elderly as helpless and dependent, on one hand, and the current positive, activist myth of all older people as healthy, vibrant, and vital, on the other.

11. Cole, Thomas R.; Gadow, Sally, Editors. What Does It Mean to Grow Old? Reflections from the Humanities. Durham, NC: Duke University Press; 1986.

Twenty essayists from a variety of fields, including ethics, try to explain the philosophical meaning attached to the aging of the American population at this point in time. Contemporary values and culture are discussed in the context of the aging phenomenon, as are our attitudes toward older people.

12. Connelly, Julia E.; DalleMura, Steven. Ethical Problems in the Medical Office. Journal of the American Medical Association; August 12, 1988; 260(6): 812-815.

This article reports on a prospective study of perceived ethical issues arising in an internal medicine office practice. The investigators found that ethical problems were more common in patients more than sixty years of age, and considerably more common in patients more than seventy years old, than in younger patients. The main ethical problems identified concerned psychological factors influencing the patient's preference, decisional capacity, informed consent, refusal of treatment, confidentiality, and the costs of care.

13. Dubler, Nancy N.; Strauss, Peter J. Ethical Dilemmas Facing Caregivers and Attorneys in Dealing with Legal, Financial, and Health-Care Decision Making. in: Aronson, Miriam K., Editor. Understanding Alzheimer's Disease. New York: Charles Scribner's Sons; 1988.

This chapter outlines a few of the ethical problems encountered by family members, attorneys, physicians, social workers, and other members of the health care team who are involved with Alzheimer's patients. These dilemmas include identifying who is the client, assessing the client's decisional capacity and the appropriateness of guardianship, privileged communications, and clashes between health care institutions and patients' rights.

14. Edel, Leon. The Artist in Old Age. Hastings Law Journal; April 1985; 15(2): 38-44.

This essay examines the ways that aging artists working in a variety of mediums--poet or painter, novelist or playwright--creatively imagine and epict the aged and the aging process. Aging artists struggle to face the ultimate truth of decline and death, and to engage in self-observation without descending into self-destruction.

15. Falk, Mark. Ethical Considerations in Representing the Elderly. South Dakota Law Review; 1991; 36(1): 54-80.

This article explores several ethical issues that may arise in providing legal services to an older client. These questions include identification of the client (the older person or the relative who brings the elder into the lawyer's office), resolving differences between an elder and family members, locating the duty of confidentiality, determining the older person's capacity to make legal decisions, and substantiating the elder's decisional capacity.

16. Foner, Nancy. Old and Frail and Everywhere Unequal. Hastings Center Report; April 1985; 15(2): 27-31.

An anthropologist examines patterns of care for the elderly in nonindustrial cultures. She explores social losses among the frail old, abandonment and killing as an extreme way to deal with the aging phenomenon, the nature of custodial care, relevant differences among the frail old, and strains--ethical, social, and psychological--and accommodation between the generations in those cultures.

17. Haas, Janet; Callahan, Daniel; Caplan, Arthur L., Editors. Casebook on Ethics and Rehabilitation Medicine. Briarcliff Manor, NY: Hastings Center; 1987.

Based on a Hastings Center project, this casebook is suitable for educational and discussion purposes concerning ethical and policy aspects of providing rehabilitation medicine to physically and mentally disabled persons.

18. Institute of Medicine, Division of Health Promotion and Disease Prevention, Committee on a National Research Agenda on Aging. Extending Life, Enhancing Life: A National Research Agenda on Aging. Lonergan, Edmund T., Editor. Washington, DC: National Academy Press; 1991.

Chapter 6 of this report sets forth a recommended national research agenda in biomedical ethics as this field relates to the health care of older persons. Research priorities identified are: ethical dilemmas involved in decision making about life-sustaining treatment, the fair allocation of health care resources, and participation in clinical research protocols by frail and elderly individuals.

19. Jecker, Nancy S., Editor. Aging and Ethics. Totowa, NJ: Humana Press; 1991.

This edited volume deals with a variety of ethical issues involving the elderly, their care, and their role in society. The book explores these concerns at four levels: the aging individual, aging and filial responsibility, distributive justice in an aging society, and philosophical reflections on aging and death.

20. Jennings, Bruce; Callahan, Daniel; Caplan, Arthur L. Ethical Challenges of Chronic Illness. Hastings Center Report; February/March 1988; 18(1): 1-16 Supplement.

This report grows out of a three year Hastings Center project on Ethics and Chronic Illness. The project was premised on the hypothesis that the special nature of chronic care and the distinctive experience of chronic illness may lead to a transformation in many pervasive assumptions about the ethics and goals of medicine. The individualistic perspective behind much of the moral discourse of bioethics and social policy does not fare well in application to chronic illness and chronic care. Concepts such as patients' rights, autonomy, and best interests need to be revised in this context. In its confrontation with chronic illness, medicine's own understanding of its goals and missions must also be redefined.

21. Kapp, Marshall B. Representing Older Persons: Ethical Challenges.

Florida Bar Journal; June 1989; 63(6): 25-30.

This article discusses ethical issues confronting an attorney who represents an older client, especially one with diminished cognitive capacity. Focus is placed on communication, conflicts of interest, confidentiality, and determinations of client capacity in the attorney/older client relationship. The attorney's role as a citizen in improving societal mechanisms and policies for serving the elderly also is acknowledged.

22. Kapp, Marshall B. Interprofessional Relationships in Geriatrics: Ethical and Legal Considerations. Gerontologist; October 1987; 27(5): 547-552.

The author explores the ethical and legal foundations for a mandate for interprofessional cooperation among the various members of a health care/social service team serving the needs of an older person. The central ethical role of the physician within the team is emphasized, as are the common barriers to effective interprofessional cooperation.

23. Kapp, Marshall B. Geriatric Medical Education: Integrating Legal and Ethical Issues. Medicine and Law; 1985; 4: 401-408.

This article advises American medical schools about including discussion of legal and ethical aspects of medical care for the elderly into the educational curriculum. Among specific considerations are appropriate teachers, particular subjects to be taught, alternative teaching methods and settings, and available teaching materials. Practical impediments to developing an effective strategy are discussed.

24. Kayser-Jones, Jeanie; Kapp, Marshall B. Advocacy for the Mentally Impaired Elderly: A Case Study Analysis. American Journal of Law and Medicine; 1989; 14(4): 353-376.

This article analyzes the role of advocates for mentally impaired nursing home residents. Focus is placed on the legal authority and ethical responsibilities of various types of potential advocates in this context. The case utilized as the framework for the discussion involved denial of appropriate medical treatment for a mentally impaired but socially intact individual. Suggestions are offered for improving the quality of long term care advocacy in a manner consistent with high ethical standards of beneficence and non-maleficence.

25. Moody, Harry R. Ethics. in: Maddox, George L., Editor. The Encyclopedia of Aging. New York: Springer Publishing Company; 1987: 224-227.

This article outlines ethical issues arising both in clinical treatment of older persons and in discussions of social policy regarding health services for the elderly. In the clinical arena, Moody emphasizes the tension between autonomy (self-determination) and paternalism (imposing limits on freedom for the purpose of protecting the patient's best interests). In the social policy realm, questions about the allocation of scarce resources and the claims of older persons are discussed.

26. Moody, Harry R. Ethics and Aging: Old Answers, New Questions. Generations; Winter 1985; 10(2): 5-9.

Philosopher Moody provides an general overview and understanding of the importance of examining, and re-examining, ethical questions in our striving for the best ways to act toward older persons. Among the specific ethical issues that he uses to illustrate why must must begin to think more creatively about practical solutions to value dilemmas are termination of medical treatment, the limits of autonomy, limits to the usefulness of the rule of law to guide conduct, and allocation of resources.

27. O'Rourke, Kevin. Developing in Younger Physicians an Ethical Perspective Toward Geriatric Patients. Journal of the American Geriatrics Society; June 1988; 36(6): 565-568.

A Catholic clergyman offers suggestions for sensitizing young physicians who treat older persons to the social and psychospiritiual needs of the patient. Development of an ethical perspective requires a process of information, example, and experience. Guiding principles in this endeavor include: (1) taking adequate time to communicate--both talk and listen--with older patients; (2) helping to comfort the dying and adjust medical interventions according to ethical norms; and (3) placing cost considerations in the background, both because more respectful care of the elderly would in itself reduce expensive and unnecessary medical treatment and because the physician's role should be one of patient advocate and not societal gatekeeper.

28. Pellegrino, Edmund D.; Sharpe, Virginia A. Medical Ethics in the Courtroom: The Need for Scrutiny. Perspectives in Biology and Medicine; Summer 1989; 32(4): 547-564.

This paper examines the way in which law and medical ethics intersect in court decisions dealing with the withholding or withdrawal of life-prolonging treatments. In examining four recent cases, the authors highlight three points of intersection: the use of medical ethical literature and testimony as evidence in the courtroom, the argumentation used by courts in assessing the merits of different ethical viewpoints, and the courts' duty to uphold the state interest in protecting the ethical integrity of the medical profession.

29. Reece, Robert D.; Faryna, Alice. Ethical Issues. in: Goldenberg, Kim; Faryna, Alice, Editors. Geriatric Medicine for the House Officer. Baltimore: Williams and Wilkins; 1990: 304-310.

This chapter outlines the humanistic qualities desirable in physicians who are caring for older patients: respect for the patient as a person, respect for the patient's autonomy, compassion, honesty (exemplified in the informed consent process), and humility. In addition, the authors discuss ethical considerations involved in treatment decisions at the end of life.

30. Schmidt, Robert M.; Kenen, Regina H. AIDS in an Aging Society: Ethical and Psychological Considerations. Generations; Fall 1989; 13(4): 36-39.

The authors contend that persons with the Acquired Immune Deficiency Syndrome (AIDS) and the elderly have much in common in terms of routine violation by society of their ethical rights to autonomy, nonmaleficence, beneficence, and justice or desert.

31. Spicker, Stuart F.: Ingman, Stanley R.; Lawson, Ian R., Editors. Ethical Dimensions of Geriatric Care: Value Conflicts for the 21st Century. Boston: Kluwer Academic Publishers Group; 1987. (Philosophy and Medicine Series; v. 25).

Emanating from a 1984 conference, this collection of essays and critical responses authored by experts from the fields of philosophy, law, medicine, nursing, and the social sciences illustrates how moral dilemmas in public policy that appear to affect only 'statistical' lives frequently impact with great force on the actual medical care of specifically 'identified' older persons. On the macro level, the chief theme is resource allocation concerning health care for the elderly. In the direct clinical realm, the central theme is the tension and interplay between the values of self-determination, dependency, and interdependence in later life.

32. Waymack, Mark H.; Taler, George A. Medical Ethics and the Elderly. Chicago: Pluribus Press; 1988.

This casebook by a philosopher and a geriatrician is a basic primer on ethical considerations in resolving the frequent tension between risk and protection for the elderly in health-related scenarios. The use of clinical hypothetical cases is illustrative of the issues presented to health care and social service providers. A strong patients' rights bias permeates the book.

33. Wetle, Terrie. Long Term Care: A Taxonomy of Issues. Generations; Winter 1985; 10(2): 30-34.

This article surveys some of the unique ethical issues that arise concerning services to older persons in long term care settings, both institutional and community-based. For the individual, these issues revolve around considerations of autonomy and independence in making life decisions. For the family, questions about appropriate expectations of support from one generation to another abound. For service providers, the proper model for their relationship with the client must be established. For the long term care delivery system as a whole, value considerations determine the fairest distribution of resources.

2
Autonomy

34. Ackermann, Joan. A Bill of Responsibilities for Nursing Home Residents. Generations; 1990; 14(Supplement): 81-82.

A fallacy in nursing home residents' bills of rights contained in federal and state regulation is in the assignment of roles. These laws require action or inaction by others. Practitioners must take the active role, residents the more passive one. Instead, the author suggests, residents should be encouraged to take an active part in the vital aspects of their living situations and to exercise responsibilities that require their action or inaction in regard to themselves, others, and their environment. This article describes and reproduces a "Bill of Resident Responsibilites" developed by one nursing home.

35. Agich, George J. Reassessing Autonomy in Long-Term Care. Hastings Center Report; November/December 1990; 20(6): 12-17.

Long term care of all sorts is required precisely because individuals experience some loss of functions that we associate with a full sense of developed adult autonomy. Philosopher Agich finds that our prevailing adversarial orientation to autonomy (the patient versus the intervenor) fails to adequately capture the mundane ethical reality of either autonomy or long term care. He proposes a contextual account that attends to the phenomenon of actual rather than ideal autonomy. Autonomy should not be dealt with as a problem reactively, but as an integral and essential aspect of caring for patients every day.

36. American Hospital Association. Policy and Statement: The Patient's Choice of Treatment Options. Chicago: AHA; February 1985; Catalogue No.

157628.

This American Hospital Association policy endorses a process of collaborative medical decisionmaking involving the patient, physician, and other members of the health care team. This process requires the patient's adequately informed consent and may involve an evaluation of the patient's capacity to make the decision in question.

37. Brody, Howard. Ethics and Therapeutic Skepticism. Journal of Family Practice; 1989; 29(6): 611-612.

Dr. Brody argues that good ethical reasoning demands rejection of two types of physician arrogance: (1) the interpersonal arrogance that physicians, not patients, should decide who will eat (even artificially) and when; and (2) the therapeutic arrogance of assuming that medical technology has the almost unlimited power to extend any life indefinitely by force-feeding fluids and nutrients.

38. Buehler, David A. Informed Consent and the Elderly: An Ethical Challenge for Critical Care Nursing. Critical Care Nursing Clinics of North America; September 1990; 2(3): 461-471.

This essay gives an overview of informed consent as an ethical ideal and its implications for critical care nursing practice. After a review of its historical roots and its potential for medical empowerment of the elderly, the concept of informed consent is analyzed in terms of its impact on the actual decisionmaking process. Finally, the ethical validity and relevance of informed consent is considered in light of both technological and organizational (role) changes affecting critical care nursing.

39. Callahan, Daniel. Autonomy: A Moral Good, Not a Moral Obsession. Hastings Center Report; October 1984; 14(5): 40-42.

Philosopher Callahan defends the principle of personal autonomy in medical decision making as necessary to protect against the excesses of paternalism. However, autonomy by itself is inadequate to good ethics, often serving as a pretext for selfishness. We need an ethics, this article urges, that will also consider our obligations to others. Callahan anticipates a future in which the medical relationship will take account not only of the individual, but also of the community with all its constraints and prohibitions.

40. Caplan, Arthur L. Let Wisdom Find a Way. Generations; Winter 1985; 10(2): 10-14.

Philosopher Caplan suggests that determinations of a patient's mental decisional capacity often represent a clash between the ideals of beneficence and autonomy. He discusses how this clash plays out in the context of assessing capacity and proposes methods for accommodating both moral values. He places special emphasis on respect for the authenticity of values, goals, and preferences expressed by the elderly. The role of the family in assisting the older person to make difficult decisions by amplifying his or her autonomy is mentioned.

41. Cassell, Eric J. Life As a Work of Art. Hastings Center Report; October 1984; 14(5): 35-37.

Dr. Cassell opines that there is no difference between a patient refusing to eat and refusing any other treatment. However, he believes that focusing exclusively on autonomy in these cases misses the larger purpose of medicine. He urges a wider inquiry and set of values, in which different decisions flow together into a single text of the patient's life.

42. Clark, Phillip G. The Philosophical Foundation of Empowerment: Implications for Geriatric Health Care Programs and Practice. Journal of Aging and Health; August 1989; 1(3): 267-285.

The author discusses the ethical implications of decision making by and on behalf of older persons. Clark notes that sometimes individuals do not wish to be empowered personally, preferring instead to relinquish decisionmaking authority to the care provider or family members. Elderly individuals and their families can benefit from support and advice when making choices concerning health care services and settings. Empowerment is a process, rather than a discrete event, representing a balance (that will vary for each person) between dependence and independence. Moral dilemmas lie at the core of striking this balance, both in terms of decisionmaking procedures and actual outcomes.

43. Clark, Phillip G. Autonomy, Personal Empowerment, and Quality of Life in Long-Term Care. Journal of Applied Gerontology; September 1988; 7(3): 279-297.

Philosopher Clark analyzes the dialectic between dependence and autonomy in advancing age, particularly when long term care services may be required to support the individual's personal needs. The need for assistance, for relying on others to meet one's basic functional requirements, does not connote a devaluation of the worth of the individual. What is required of service providers is a sensitivity to how each person strikes the balance between dependence and independence in his or her own life.

44. Clark, Phillip G. Individual Autonomy, Cooperative Empowerment, and Planning for Long-Term Care Decision Making. Journal of Aging Studies; 1987; 1(1): 65-76.

This article first outlines the major features of the concept of client empowerment as it relates to individuals assuming more responsibility for their own health care and health-related decisions. Second, Clark develops the emerging concept of client autonomy as an ethical framework within which we can gain a better understanding of what planning for long term care decisions should entail. Third, the author considers the implications of this framework for how planning should be encouraged and conducted. This includes the development of the concept of cooperative empowerment applied in both the direct service and the social policy contexts.

45. Cohen, Elias S. The Elderly Mystique: Constraints on the Autonomy of the Elderly With Disabilities. Gerontologist; June 1988; 28(Supplement): 24-31.

Cohen suggests that older physically disabled persons frequently are granted very little personal autonomy because their potential for active involvement in choices is automatically underestimated both by themselves and others. He wishes to dispel this dependency myth, and looks to the Women's Movement, Mentally Retarded Individual Rights Movement, and Independent Living Movement for lessons applicable to the elderly.

46. Cohen, Elias S. Autonomy and Paternalism: Two Goals in Conflict.

Law, Medicine & Health Care; September 1985; 13(4): 145-150.

Cohen discusses the moral tensions between autonomy and beneficence as these principles are applied in practice to decision making about health care and human services for older persons. He discusses the claims-based approach to rights, under which individuals attain benefits or entitlements only if they have the vigor, independence, and knowledge to demand them. Cohen would reject the adversarial due process approach to elder rights in favor of a theory of limited paternalism supplemented by a service system that potentiates and enhances the autonomy of those who may be acquiescent and defeated.

47. Cohen, Uriel; Weisman, Gerald D. Experimental Design to Maximize Autonomy for Older Adults With Cognitive Impairments. Generations; 1990; 14(Supplement): 75-78.

A potentially significant, but often overlooked, resource in efforts to enhance the autonomy of older persons residing in institutions is the physical environment in which they live. Research points to multiple ways in which environmental design can contribute to the maintenance and maximization of autonomy. Recently, research and design efforts have examined environments for older adults with cognitive impairments, especially those resulting from dementia. Based upon this work, this article presents a framework for the definition of autonomy within an environmental context along with a set of broad principles for design.

48. Collopy, Bart J. Autonomy in Long Term Care: Some Crucial Distinctions. Gerontologist; June 1988; 28(Supplement): 10-17.

A philosopher provides a conceptual discursion into the various basic issues that the principle of personal autonomy in long term care settings may raise. He utilizes case examples to illustrate the different forms in which the operationalizing of autonomy can present ethical complexities.

49. Collopy, Bart J. Ethical Dimensions of Autonomy in Long-Term Care. Generations; 1990; 14(Supplement): 9-12.

In the ethics of long term care, autonomy often is a conflict-laden value. Philosopher Collopy analyzes a number of fundamental concepts that run throughout a discussion of personal autonomy in long term care environments. Among the concepts analyzed are evaluation of decisional capacity, how present freedom can work against future freedom, the distinction between decisional autonomy and autonomy of execution--that is, the difference between doing for the elderly and deciding for them, the distinction between direct and delegated autonomy, and the polarity between negative (i.e., being left alone without interference) and positive (i.e., being provided with resources and assistance) rights.

50. Conrad, Peter. The Noncompliant Patient in Search of Autonomy. Hastings Center Report; August 1987; 17(4): 15-17.

A sociologist looks at the ethical implications of chronically ill patients who fail to comply with their physicians' recommendations for treatment. Conrad interprets such behavior in terms of a quest for autonomy and independence, rather than deviance or irrationality.

51. Culver, Charles M.; Gert, Bernard. The Inadequacy of Incompetence. Milbank Quarterly; 1990; 68(4): 619-643.

The authors develop the argument that capacity (they use the term "competence") to make medical decisions is neither a necessary nor a sufficient condition for determining when it is morally justified to overrule a patient's treatment refusal. It is not a necessary condition because it is morally justified to overrule some patients who are competent to refuse. It is not a sufficient condition because the fact that a patient lacks capacity to refuse does not by itself morally justify overruling his or her treatment refusal.

52. Drane, James F. The Many Faces of Competency. Hastings Center Report; April 1985; 15(2): 17-21.

Philosopher Drane analyzes the concept of mental capacity (competency) to make medical decisions. He advocates use of a sliding scale under which, as the medical decision itself (the task) changes in complexity, the standards for judging capacity to perform the task should change also.

53. Ende, Jack; Kazis, Lewis; Ash, Arlene; Moskowitz, Mark A. Measuring Patients' Desire for Autonomy: Decision Making and Information-Seeking Preferences Among Medical Patients. Journal of General Internal Medicine; January-February 1989; 4(1): 23-30.

The authors tested an instrument they developed to measure patients' preferences on two dimensions of autonomy: (1) desire to make medical decisions and (2) desire to be informed of medical details. The study found that generally older patients had less desire than younger patients to make decisions and to be informed, preferring to defer to physician authority. The article cautions clinicians, however, that they must get to know each patient as an individual to assess his or her desires regarding both dimensions of autonomy.

54. Erde, Edmund L.; Nadal, Evan C.; Scholl, Theresa O. On Truth Telling and the Diagnosis of Alzheimer's Disease. Journal of Family Practice; April 1988; 26(4): 401-404.

These researchers surveyed patients who were waiting to see their physicians about whether they would want to be told a diagnosis of Alzheimer's disease. The affirmative response exceeded ninety percent. The article argues that a policy of truthfulness with patients (and with families, where authorized to receive information by the patient) in this context is compelled under both consequentialist (i.e., looking at outcomes) and teleological (i.e., concentrating on rights) ethical theories. An accompanying editorial by Howard Brody and Tom Tomlinson (pages 404-406) raise some conceptual and methodological concerns about this study.

55. Faden, Ruth R.; Beauchamp, Tom L. A History and Theory of Informed Consent. New York: Oxford University Press; 1986.

This book is a comprehensive study of the historical roots and conceptual underpinnings of the informed consent doctrine. The ethicist authors draw an important distinction between patient consent to care that is minimally legally effective, on one hand, and a consent process that truly promotes the ethical value of personal autonomy, on the other. Implications for the provider/patient relationship are drawn.

56. Gutheil, Thomas G.; Appelbaum, Paul S. The Substituted Judgment

Approach: Its Difficulties and Paradoxes in Mental Health Settings. Law, Medicine & Health Care; April 1985; 13(2): 61-64.

Two psychiatrists argue that relying on a process of substituted judgment to make medical decisions for a decisionally incapacitated patient (that is, trying to determine what the patient would want if he or she were currently capable of making and expressing autonomous choices) is ethically and pragmatically problematic. The authors contend that, in the absence of an unambiguous indication of the incapacitated patient's desires, a best interests approach should be taken. Further, when the treatment at issue has a good probability of restoring the person's decisional capacity, they would favor a presumption that treatment is in the patient's best interests. Treatment that can restore autonomy should be encouraged by society.

57. Handler, Joel F. Community Care for the Frail Elderly: A Theory of Empowerment. Ohio State Law Journal; 1989; 50: 541-560.

The author argues that simply giving the frail elderly a set of legal rights will not assure their autonomy, because legal rights are not self-executing. Instead, he proposes empowering older persons to control the design and delivery of their own care plans--in the community and in institutions--by affording them the financial ability (e.g., through vouchers), information, and range of alternatives to select, hire, and fire their service providers.

58. Hardwig, John. What About the Family? Hastings Center Report; March/April 1990; 20(2): 5-10.

This article argues that the family has a strong ethical stake in medical decisionmaking for both mentally competent and incompetent patients. An overbroad concentration on the principle of individual patient autonomy must be balanced against the impact of medical decisions on the legitimate rights and interests of the patient's family members.

59. Hegeman, Carol; Tobin, Sheldon. Enhancing the Autonomy of Mentally Impaired Nursing Home Residents. Gerontologist; June 1988; 28(Supplement): 71-75.

This mail survey of non-profit nursing homes identified a variety of autonomy-enhancing programs for cognitively impaired residents. These initiatives included special resident programming, structural and environmental adaptations, staff training, family programming, staff deployment, and ethics initiatives (e.g., lecture series). The underlying goals of these various strategies are discussed.

60. Hennessy, Catherine H. Autonomy and Risk: The Role of Client Wishes in Community-Based Long-Term Care. Gerontologist; October 1989; 29(5): 633-639.

This study examined the extent to which older clients' choices are incorporated into care planning within a large, prepaid, comprehensive social health maintenance organization. As organizational resource capacity became strained and/or the risk to a client's safety increased, the plan's case management team would give shorter shrift to the client's expressed preferences in the care plan. That is, tradeoffs were made to benefit the agency and its membership as a whole.

61. Hofland, Brian F. Autonomy in Long term Care: Background Issues and a Programmatic Response. Gerontologist; June 1988; 28(Supplement): 3-9.

In this introduction to a special supplement, the Vice-President of the Retirement Research Foundation explains the importance of blending the perspectives of ethics, law, and psychosocial research in a meaningful study of the nature and operation of autonomy in long term care. He then outlines the background and goals of the RRF's four year Personal Autonomy in Long Term Care Initiative.

62. Hughes, Tom E.; Larson, Lon N. Patient Involvement in Health Care: A Procedural Justice Viewpoint. Medical Care; March 1991; 29(3): 297-303.

This article presents a conception of procedural justice as a theoretical base to support increasing calls for patient involvement in health care decision making. Procedural justice views individuals as being concerned not only with the outcomes of a decision, but also with the fairness of the process used in making the decision.

63. Jameton, Andrew. In the Borderlands of Autonomy: Responsibility in

Long Term Care Facilities. Gerontologist; June 1988; 28(Supplement): 18-23.

Jameton discusses the notion of personal responsibilities of nursing home residents as they correlate to the rights encompassed in the principle of individual autonomy. Responsibilities and rights are mutually supportive in this environment, he suggests, and providers and policymakers should encourage, within appropriate limits, the responsible effectuation of each.

64. Jecker, Nancy S. The Role of Intimate Others in Medical Decision Making. Gerontologist; February 1990; 30(1): 65-71.

This article discusses the ethical implications of shared decision making among the older person and his/her family. Older persons usually do not function as lone, isolated individuals making completely autonomous choices, but rather as part of a community in which the family is the basic unit. Relying on family members or friends to assist in medical decision making actually enhances the patient's autonomy.

65. Jecker, Nancy S.; Self, Donnie J. Medical Ethics in the 21st Century: Respect for Autonomy in Care of the Elderly Patient. Journal of Critical Care; March 1991; 6(1): 46-51.

This article reviews the ethical principle of autonomy in the context of a rapidly aging patient population. Jecker and Self look especially at five areas in which autonomy is crucially at stake for geriatric patients, and suggest ways in which self-determination can be sustained and safeguarded: (1) advance directives, (2) mental decisional capacity, (3) gender bias, (4) medication, and (5) special considerations in home care and nursing home settings.

66. Kane, Rosalie A.; Freeman, Iris C.; Caplan, Arthur L.; Aroskar, Mila A.; Urv-Wong, E. Kristi. Everyday Autonomy in Nursing Homes. Generations; 1990; 14(Supplement): 69-71.

In the nursing home, many issues besides life and death medical decision making demand ethical reflection. An important focus is everyday life in the facility, and how to define and promote appropriate autonomy for nursing home residents on an ongoing basis. Using a blend of empirical study, ethical inquiry, and policy analysis, the authors explore this topic systematically.

67. Kapp, Marshall B. Medical Empowerment of the Elderly. Hastings Center Report; July/August 1989; 19(4): 5-7.

Empowering the elderly to make their own medical decisions regarding medical care is a noble social, political, and ethical cause. However, the author warns, some older people may not wish to make ultimate decisions for themselves, and some may even be reluctant to participate in the decisionmaking process. Society must guard against excessive preoccupation with self-determination that might, ironically, deny the elderly their autonomy by forcing it upon them.

68. Kapp, Marshall B. Enforcing Patient Preferences: Linking Payment for Medical Care to Informed Consent. Journal of the American Medical Association; April 7, 1989; 261(13): 1935-1928.

To give enforcement teeth to the ethical concept of patient decisionmaking autonomy and the legal doctrine of informed consent, particularly in the context of unwanted life-sustaining medical interventions, the author proposes that providers not be financially compensated for services provided unless they were agreed to by the patient or an authorized proxy. Linking payment for medical care to informed consent would enhance patient autonomy and conserve scarce medical resources.

69. Kapp, Marshall B. Family Decision-Making for Nursing Home Residents: Legal Mechanisms and Ethical Underpinnings. Theoretical Medicine; 1987; 8: 259-273.

This article looks at the question of surrogate or proxy medical decisionmaking by families on behalf of mentally incapable nursing home residents. Discussed are methods of delegation of authority from a resident to a family member: by advance planning; by operation of statute, regulation, or judicial precedent; by custom or convention; or by court order. The ethical principles underlying both the selection of a proxy decisionmaker and the making of specific treatment choices is explicated.

70. Kapp, Marshall B. Legal and Ethical Aspects of Health Care for the

Elderly. Medical Times; October 1986; 114(10): 45-51.

This article outlines some ethical and legal issues that arise in everyday geriatric practice. Under the heading of decisionmaking fall considerations of informed consent, mental competency, familial authority, guardianship, advance health care planning, and truth telling. Malpractice issues are mentioned briefly, as are the ethical and legal concerns raised by health care cost containment efforts.

71. Kapp, Marshall B. Legal and Ethical Issues in Resident Independence. American Health Care Association Journal; March 1983; 9(2): 22-25.

This article examines ethical and legal implications of allowing nursing home residents to have freedom of mobility. Principles of autonomy versus beneficence may conflict, and the nursing home's fears about potential liability for injury befalling an unrestrained resident complicate the picture. The author offers tentative advice for reconciling these conflicts in a way that promotes resident rights, resident protections from harm, and the legal welfare of the institution.

72. Katz, Jay. The Silent World of Doctor and Patient. New York: Free Press; 1984.

Dr. Katz explores the dynamics of physician/patient communication and analyzes why physicians frequently are reluctant to share information--especially concerning medical uncertainty--with the patient. The book's goal is to bring the everyday practice of informed consent more into line with lofty ethical principles of patient autonomy and respect and legal requirements that purport to enforce those sentiments.

73. Lako, Christiaan J.; Lindenthal, Jacob J. Confidentiality in Medical Practice. Journal of Family Practice; 1990; 31(2): 167-170.

This article reports on a mail survey of general practitioners and family physicians designed to use hypothetical vignettes to elicit physician attitudes regarding confidentiality of patient information. A particularly strong reluctance was found among physicians to divulge information to other physicians. More physicians appeared willing to disclose information to relatives of the patient without the patient's consent.

74. Lichtenberg, Peter A.; Strzepek, Deborah M. Assessments of Institutionalized Dementia Patients' Competencies to Participate in Intimate Relationships. Gerontologist; February 1990; 30(1): 117-120.

Long term care institutions must develop policies that deal with situations of demented residents who wish to engage in sexual relations within the institution. This article describes how one institution has worked through the ethical tensions presented by this situation, in developing and implementing a policy that balances the various ethical principles at stake.

75. Lidz, Charles W.; Appelbaum, Paul S.; Meisel, Alan. Two Models of Implementing Informed Consent. Archives of Internal Medicine; June 1988; 148(6): 1385-1389.

Compliance with the bare legal requirements of informed consent may be achieved by what the authors call the event model, which treats informed consent as a separate procedure to be performed once for each discrete medical procedure. However, this article maintains, a process model which intertwines informing the patient into an ongoing physician/patient dialogue about diagnosis and treatment better approaches the ethical ideals undergirding the informed consent doctrine.

76. Lidz, Charles W.; Arnold, Robert M. Institutional Constraints on Autonomy. Generations; 1990; 14(Supplement): 65-68.

This article summarizes an observational study of how the institutional structures of long term care settings affect elderly residents' autonomy. The authors suggest that, instead of equating autonomy with absolute independence, we must recognize individuals within a social and historical context. Rather than asking whether one's choice is influenced by others and assuming that all such influences inhibit autonomy, the proper question is how institutional factors affect one's actions and whether these influences subvert one's control, reasoning, or identification with one's own actions. Institutional structures that support the development and fulfillment of the individual's freely chosen commitments and life plans are autonomy enhancing; those that do the reverse impede autonomy.

77. Lo, Bernard. Assessing Decision-Making Capacity. Law, Medicine & Health Care; Fall 1990; 18(3): 193-201.

Physician Lo explores the practical significance of competence and capacity for medical decision making, legal standards for competence, clinical standards for determining decisional capacity, the role of mental status testing and psychiatric evaluation, and the ethical ramifications of disagreements between physicians and patients and of the need to make decisions on behalf of incapacitated patients.

78. Lohr, Kathleen N.; Donaldson, Molla S. Assuring Quality of Care for the Elderly. Law, Medicine & Health Care; Fall 1990; 18(3): 244-253.

This article discusses a recent report of the Institute of Medicine/National Academy of Sciences on methods of assuring quality of care for older persons under the Medicare program. The authors note that any quality assurance program is challenged to devise ways to consider the values and preferences of individual patients for different types of health care and the expected results of that care. This is especially difficult for a public program, which must take account of broader social values and preferences that may conflict with the wishes of at least some portion of the patient population. Regulatory models may not be able to resolve these dilemmas fully, and much responsibility will fall back to the professional community. Yet health practitioners face difficult predicaments in balancing traditional obligations of beneficence and non-maleficence with newer notions of patient autonomy and distributive justice.

79. Mazur, Dennis J. What Should Patients Be Told Prior to a Medical Procedure? Ethical and Legal Perspectives on Medical Informed Consent. American Journal of Medicine; December 1986; 81(12): 1051-1054.

This brief essay is a basic, straightforward exposition of the law of medical informed consent and the ethical principles that undergird the legal rules. Dr. Mazur discusses pragmatic concerns for the physician who must fulfill the ethical and legal mandates of the informed consent doctrine.

80. McCrary, S. Van; Walman, A. Terry. Procedural Paternalism in Competency Determination. Law, Medicine & Health Care; Spring-Summer

1990; 18(1-2): 108-113.

This paper presents and discusses a case exemplifying a particular problem that can arise in the process of evaluating a patient's capacity to make his or her own autonomous medical decisions. The authors argue that once the evaluation process has been initiated, the bureaucratic procedural forces, combined with the inconsistencies between ethical and legal theory and actual practice, in many cases gather sufficient momentum that they are impossible to halt short of a determination of decisional incapacity. McCrary and Walman dub this phenomenon "procedural paternalism.".

81. Moody, Harry R. From Informed Consent to Negotiated Consent. Gerontologist; June 1988; 28(Supplement): 64-70.

Traditional notions of decisionmaking within long term care as representing a harsh tension between unbridled individual choice, on one hand, and provider paternalism, on the other, are attacked here on practical and ethical grounds. Philosopher Moody, bolstered by qualitative interviews with physicians, nurses, and social workers in nursing homes, argues that a continuum of interventions somewhere between isolated individual choice and completely ignoring the patient's wishes should be pursued as more realistic and more protective of true patient autonomy.

82. Morison, Robert S. The Biological Limits of Autonomy. Hastings Center Report; October 1984; 14(5): 43-49.

This essay traces the recent preoccupation of medical ethics with the protection of individual rights as exercised through autonomy or self-determination in decision making. Morison is concerned that this emphasis ignores the biological reality of humans as social beings dependent upon membership in a community. He urges medical ethics to account better for this reality.

83. Norman, Alison J. Rights and Risk: A Discussion Document on Civil Liberty in Old Age. London, England: National Corporation for the Care of Old People; 1980.

This monograph explores the philosophical and practical tensions between recognition of the right to make personal choices--including choices that entail serious risks--and the role of society in protecting vulnerable older persons who are physically or mentally disabled. The relevance of finite resources as an influence on this tension is discussed. Chapters of special interest concern compulsory care, human rights and nursing care, and treatment decisions near the end of life.

84. Ouslander, Joseph G.; Osterweil, Dan; Morley, John. Medical Care in the Nursing Home. New York: McGraw-Hill, Inc.; 1991.

Chapter 25 of this volume focuses on important ethical issues faced by physicians who care for nursing home residents and suggests strategies to deal with these issues. Specific areas of attention are decisionmaking capacity and informed consent, decisions on intensity of treatment, institutional policies, advance directives, and institutional ethics committees.

85. Pratt, Clara C.; Jones, Laura L.; Shin, Hwa-Yong; Walker, Alexis J. Autonomy and Decision Making Between Single Older Women and Their Caregiving Daughters. Gerontologist; December 1989; 29(6): 792-797.

This survey of single older women living in the community confirms the findings of previous studies that many such persons usually confront difficult life decisions, especially those regarding health care, not as isolated, atomistic individuals, but rather with the support and active involvement of adult daughters. The influence of adult daughters in terms of the older person's autonomy and well-being, and hence how we conceptualize the nature of informed consent for the type of person observed here, is discussed.

86. President's Commission for the Study of Ethical Problems in Medicine and Biomedical and Behavioral Research. Making Health Care Decisions: The Ethical and Legal Implications of Informed Consent in the Patient-Practitioner Relationship. Washington, DC: U.S. Government Printing Office; October 1982.

This report analyzes in depth the ethical implications of the doctrine of informed consent. It explores the underlying values, the concept of informed consent as a shared and active process, the importance of provider/patient communication, the elements of decisional capacity and voluntariness, practical innovations, and aspects of professional outlook and behavior that impact on informed consent being achieved. The final part deals with special ethical considerations that arise where the patient lacks decisionmaking capacity.

87. Quill, Timothy E.; Townsend, Penelope. Bad News: Delivery, Dialogue, and Dilemmas. Archives of Internal Medicine; March 1991; 151: 463-468.

Using a narrative from an actual patient encounter, a physician and a nurse discuss goals and techniques for sharing disastrous news with patients in as sensitive and humane a manner as possible. The clinician's obligations regarding follow-up to the delivery of the bad news are also analyzed.

88. Quill, Timothy E. Recognizing and Adjusting to Barriers in Doctor-Patient Communication. Annals of Internal Medicine; July 1, 1989; 111(1): 51-57.

Dr. Quill identifies potential barriers (one of which is age) to effective physician/patient communications, which frequently impair the outcome of medical treatment. The paper advises how to negotiate with the patient a workable resolution to these barriers that will enhance the therapeutic relationship.

89. Ratzan, Richard M. Informed Consent from the Mentally Incompetent Elderly. Postgraduate Medicine; October 1986; 80(5): 81-88.

Dr. Ratzan examines the physician's ethical challenges and duties regarding medical decisionmaking where the older patient is decisionally incapable. He explores the definition of mental incompetence, methods for evaluating it, alternatives to the patient's valid informed consent, and ways in which the physician can help presently competent patients to plan for possible future mental incapacity.

90. Rettig, Richard A.; Levinsky, Norman G., Editors. Kidney Failure and the Federal Government. Institute of Medicine, Committee for the Study of the Medicare End-Stage Renal Disease Program. Washington, DC: National Academy Press; 1991.

In 1972, the Medicare statute was amended to provide an entitlement to kidney dialysis and transplantation services. The current patient population served by this entitlement now averages sixty years old, with an even greater proportion of older patients expected in the future. Chapter 3 of this report discusses three major ethical concerns as they apply to End-Stage Renal Disease patients: patient acceptance criteria for treatment, criteria for the termination of treatment, and ethical questions arising for caregivers who deal with problem (e.g., noncompliant, self-destructive, abusive) patients. The committee felt that these ethical issues are properly the domain of patients, families, physicians, and other caregivers, and that there is no role for federal legislative or regulatory activity in this realm.

91. Schouten, Ronald. Informed Consent: Resistance and Reappraisal. Critical Care Medicine; December 1989; 17(12): 1359-1361.

This editorial endorses the plea for compliance with the ethical spirit, as well as the legal letter, of the informed consent doctrine. Attorney/physician Schouten suggests that minimalistic, formalistic compliance is neither good patient care nor effective defensive medicine, while sincere communication with the patient and/or family is both clinically therapeutic and legally preventative.

92. Smith, Mindy A.; Green, Lee A.; Ward, Paul. Aggressive Therapy in the Care of the Critically Ill Patient. Journal of Family Practice; 1987; 25(2): 119-124.

This report of a family practice grand rounds presents a discussion of the ethical issues surrounding a case of an elderly women admitted to the hospital in cardiogenic shock who, despite a grave prognosis, wishes for all possible intervention. The respective roles of the family, attendingphysician, and consultants in caring for this patient are considered, including early resuscitation decisions, the use of mechanical ventilation and continuous positive airway pressure by mask, and establishing decisional capacity.

93. Sprung, Charles L.; Winick, Bruce J. Informed Consent in Theory and Practice: Legal and Medical Perspectives on the Informed Consent Doctrine and a Proposed Reconceptualization. Critical Care Medicine; December 1989; 17(12): 1346-1354.

This article is an exposition of the law of medical informed consent and the ethical principles forming the basis for the legal rules. The authors, a physician and an attorney, emphasize the importance of a good informed consent process for purposes of fostering the physician/patient relationship and therapeutic benefit for the patient, as well as for defensive risk management. They propose more flexibility in meeting the requirements of the informed consent doctrine, particularly endorsing the idea of a sliding scale for assessing decisional capacity.

94. Stanley, Barbara, Editor. Geriatric Psychiatry: Ethical and Legal Issues. Washington, DC: American Psychiatric Press; 1985.

This monograph presents five essays that deal with particular ethical, legal, and clinical problems that arise in the context of providing health care services to older persons and their families in the psychiatric setting. Informed consent and elderly patient participation in research protocols are among the specific topics discussed.

95. Stanley, Barbara; Stanley, Michael; Guido, Jeannine; Garvin, Lynn. The Functional Competency of Elderly at Risk. Gerontologist; June 1988; 28(Supplement): 53-58.

This article describes standards of decisionmaking capacity and an investigation by psychologists into the functional ability of older depressed and cognitively impaired mental patients to meet those standards. The investigators found decisional capacity problems in the older cognitively impaired cohort, and recommend strategies for enhancing the autonomy of members of this group in the consent process.

96. Streib, Gordon F.; Folts, W. Edward; LaGreca, Anthony J. Autonomy, Power, and Decision-Making in Thirty-Six Retirement Communities. Gerontologist; August 1985; 25(4): 403-409.

Through conducting interviews and reviewing documents, these sociologists drew case histories of thirty-six retirement communities. They found that, for some residents of these communities, exercising power and autonomous decisionmaking authority was an important opportunity and highly valued. For most older residents, though, there was a desire to retain the right to act autonomously if necessary but a preference that day-to-day decisions about community governance be made by others.

97. Thomasma, David C. Quality of Life Judgments and Medical Indications. Quality of Life and Cardiovascular Care; Spring 1986; 2(3): 113-118.

Philosopher Thomasma explores the impact of changing medical practices and sophisticated technologies on traditional assumptions regarding beneficence, the ethical principle teaching us to help and protect others.   He raises challenges to the standard beneficence doctrine, explains why quality of life and medical indications judgments are imperative, and proposes axioms for aid in making such judgments in the future.

98. Tomlinson, Tom; Howe, Kenneth; Notman, Mark; Rossmiller, Diane. An Empirical Study of Proxy Consent for Elderly Persons. Gerontologist; February 1990; 30(1): 54-64.

In this study, elderly persons and their relatives were asked for medical treatment preferences in the context of several hypothetical scenarios. Relatives who were asked to make a substituted judgment (i.e., to decide as they thought the older person herself would decide) came much closer to matching the older person's actual choice than did physicians or relatives who were asked to decide according to their own judgment of which treatment was in the patient's best interests.   This study supports the use of proxy decisionmaking for difficult medical choices as a matter of patient autonomy, but only where the proxy is held to a substituted judgment standard.

99. Tymchuk, Alexander J.; Ouslander, Joseph G.; Rahbar, Bita; Fitten, Jaime. Medical Decision-Making among Elderly People in Long Term Care. Gerontologist; June 1988; 28(Supplement): 59-63.

These investigators presented informed consent information on high and low risk medical interventions to older nursing home residents in three different formats.   They found comprehension much superior when information was presented in a simplified or storybook format, rather than using the standard approach.   Ethical and practice implications are drawn regarding the meaningful participation of older patients in the consent process.

100. U.S. Congress, Office of Technology Assessment. Losing a Million Minds: Confronting the Tragedy of Alzheimer's Disease and Other Dementias. Washington, DC: U.S. Government Printing Office; April 1987;

OTA-BA-323.

Chapter 5 of this report covers ethical aspects of making medical decisions for persons with dementia. Specific topics addressed include determinations of decisional capacity, methods of identifying surrogate decision makers, decisionmaking criteria, problems with relying on surrogates' decisions, and decisions concerning the enrollment of demented persons in research protocols. A set of options for developing public policy on these issues is presented.

101. Veatch, Robert M. Autonomy's Temporary Triumph. Hastings Center Report; October 1984; 14(5): 38-40.

Philosopher Veatch applauds the principle of individual autonomy in medical decision making as necessary to counterbalance the tradition of paternalism that has gone unchallenged for years. However, as medical ethics matures and learns to take account of the community also, he asserts, it must adjust to handle social as well as individual ethical questions.

102. Waitzkin, Howard B. Research on Doctor-Patient Communication: Implications for Practice. Internist; August 1986; 27(7): 7-10.

Waitzkin reviews social scientific research on the nature of physician/patient communication. Age is one of the social structural barriers that inhibits effective communication in clinical practice. The author suggests that nonverbal communications are important, and often neglected, in medical encounters. Moreover, to the extent that it presents a problem to communication, the interrogative mode of the medical history deserves reconsideration.

103. Weinstock, Robert; Copelan, Russell; Bagheri, Abbas. Competence to Give Informed Consent for Medical Procedures. Bulletin of the American Academy of Psychiatry and the Law; 1984; 12(2): 117-125.

The authors critique the process of determining mental decisionmaking capacity for patients who have been referred to a psychiatrist. They argue that many patients so referred--mainly because they have refused to follow a physician's recommendation--are more decisionally capable than is ordinarily assumed.

104. Welch, D. Don. Walking in Their Shoes: Paying Respect to Incompetent Patients. Vanderbilt Law Review; 1989; 42: 1617-1640.

This essay focuses on how third-party decisions regarding consent to medical treatment should be made, and concludes that considerations of substituted judgment should be given a clear priority over considerations that traditionally have been labeled the patient's best interests. The model of informed consent that emerges from this discussion is very individual patient oriented. Underlying this approach is an image of a covenant between doctor and patient that contrasts with the traditional medical model.

105. Wolf, Susan M. Conflict Between Doctor and Patient. Law, Medicine & Health Care; Fall/Winter 1988; 16(3-4): 197-203.

Wolf argues that the avoidance of conflict between physician and patient over treatment decisions often is purchased through persistent silence and automatic acquiescence, whereas the physician/patient relationship should be characterized by an open and vigorous communication of information, goals, values, and approaches. Wolf argues that such communication is desirable, even (perhaps especially) if conflict develops. She uses the issue of medical futility as an example of an important topic that physicians have been afraid to raise in conversations with their patients.

3

Financing

106. Agich, George J. Rationing and Professional Autonomy. Law, Medicine & Health Care; Spring-Summer 1990; 18(1-2): 77-84.

Philosopher Agich examines the relationship between professional authority and health care rationing and the claim that rationing, especially rationing brought about by changes in the way health care is financed, threaten to undermine professional authority. Agich believes that, thus far at least, most physician anguish about the advent of health care rationing has been motivated primarily by the medical profession's stake in perpetuating the inflationary and inequitable prevailing fee-for-service, third party payment system for medical care.

107. American Geriatrics Society Public Policy Committee. Equitable Distribution of Limited Medical Resources. Journal of the American Geriatrics Society; November 1989; 37(11): 1063-1064.

This AGS public policy statement urges that chronological age not be used as a sole, arbitrary criterion for limiting particular kinds of medical care. Instead, rationing criteria should include likelihood of benefit, burden, prognosis, quality of life, and patient preferences. Relatively higher health expenditures for the elderly may be justified, since need is greatest in this group. Health care resources used in caring for older persons must be fairly divided among all their different types of health needs, including supportive, preventive, and rehabilitative services, as well as toward curative efforts.

108. Avorn, Jerry. Benefit and Cost Analysis in Geriatric Care: Turning Age

Discrimination into Health Policy. New England Journal of Medicine; 1984; 310: 1294-1301.

The author explains how the popular methodologies of cost/benefit analysis in health care will inevitably become a hidden, unfair method of rationing potentially beneficial health care according to patient age. He urges resistance to this approach to cost containment and what he sees as its ethically unacceptable consequences.

109. Barry, Robert L.; Bradley, Gerard V., Editors. Set No Limits: A Rebuttal to Daniel Callahan's Proposal to Limit Health Care for the Elderly. Urbana, IL: University of Illinois Press; 1991.

This collection of ethical, legal, philosophical, economic, religious, and political science essays attacks, from a politically conservative perspective, proposals to ration potentially beneficial health care according to the chronological age of prospective patients.

110. Battin, Margaret P. Age Rationing and the Just Distribution of Health Care: Is There a Duty to Die? Ethics; January 1987; 97(2): 317-40.

This article examines proposals for health care rationing according to the patient's chronological age in the light of current issues concerning distributive justice in health care. It asks whether there is any moral warrant to this position and what consequences such a policy would have for the health care of the aged. Philosopher Battin ends up arguing strongly against current age-based rationing proposals as probably unnecessary and certainly unjust.

111. Bayer, Ronald. Ethical Challenges in the Movement for Home Health Care. Generations; Winter 1986-87; 11(2): 44-47.

Philosopher Bayer looks globally at the current and projected need for home care services and the shortage and maldistribution of these services today. He asks what social or distributive justice demands in the provision of home care services, and how much of the burden of paying for such care should be borne by those of diminished capacity and in ill health, versus their families and the government. He argues for a larger public sector role.

112. Bayer, Ronald. Coping With Cost Containment. Generations; Winter 1985; 10(2): 39-42.

Bayer looks at the ethical ramifications of the recent altered sociopolitical climate of financing health care for the elderly. He is worried about the adverse impact of societal emphasis on cost containment, in terms of shifting more financial responsibility back to patients and families, limiting provider payments and thus sowing disincentives to serving the elderly, and constraints on the development and dissemination of advanced technology.

113. Bayer, Ronald. Will the First Medicare Generation Be the Last? Hastings Center Report; June 1984; 14(3): 17.

This essay reflects on the ethical and social underpinnings of the Medicare program for financing health care for older persons, and fears that these underpinnings may be slipping today.

114. Berenson, Robert A. A Physician's Reflections. Hastings Center Report; January/February 1989; 19(1): 12-15.

Dr. Berenson reviews the ethical implications of utilization review in the modern health care picture. He reluctantly concludes that, given the weaknesses of the traditional fee-for-service system and attempts to shift substantial risk-sharing to providers, the Medicare model of hospital prospective payment and utilization review is the best option for balancing the medical needs of individual patients with the interests of society to have health care costs constrained. The adversarial model, with physicians representing particular patients against the health care financing system, is preferable to existing alternative models.

115. Binstock, Robert H.; Post, Stephen G., Editors. Too Old for Health Care? Controversies in Medicine, Law, Economics, and Ethics. Baltimore: Johns Hopkins University Press; 1991.

In this book, a group of professionals from the fields of ethics, economics, law, gerontology, and medicine argue that limiting beneficial medical care solely on the basis of the patient's age cannot be justified on ethical, political, or financial grounds. The authors explore alternative approaches to the problem of health care cost containment. They discuss topics ranging from the economics of geriatric care to the use of medical technology for older patients, from legal and religious views on rationing health care to ways of establishing equitable public policies.

116. Blaise, Michael. Rationing Health Care to the Elderly. University of Houston Health Law News; December 1989; 3(3): 2-4.

This article looks at the ethical ramifications of rationing scarce health care resources based on age. Specific types of rationing discussed are: social worth allocation, market determined rationing, rationing according to medical criteria, the egalitarian approach, aresponsible or covert rationing, and procedural due process rationing. The author argues against age-based beneficial health care rationing schemes to contain costs.

117. Bone, Roger C.; Elpern, Ellen H. Honoring Patient Preferences and Rationing Intensive Care: Are These Compatible Goals? Archives of Internal ° Medicine; June 1991; 151(6): 1061-1063.

The authors warn that we are on a collision course between patient and family expectations of limitless intensive care to achieve even marginal benefits for critically ill persons, medical realities that involve limits to the benefits that actually can be reached through providing intensive care, and the growing scarcity of economic resources. If individuals and society do not reconcile patient and family expectations with medical and economic realities soon, an ethical disaster is predicted.

118. Bortz, Walter M. II. The Trajectory of Dying: Functional Status in the Last Year of Life. Journal of the American Geriatrics Society; February 1990; 38(2): 146-150.

This study of functional status in the last year of life casts into major question the suggestion that age be appropriated as a logical handle for allocation of scarce medical resources. The findings suggest that medical practice is already addressing the allocation of high cost resources (i.e., hospitals) according to a more defensible criterion, namely, the patient's level of functioning.

119. Brazil, Percy. Should Doctors Cut Costs at the Bedside? Cost Effective Care is Better Care. Hastings Center Report; February 1986; 16(1): 7-8.

Dr. Brazil contends that American physicians today have an obligation to consider cost implications in daily decision making about patient care, and to engage in actions to conserve limited health care resources. By being cost effective in making treatment choices in the hospital, the patient's home, the nursing facility, and in recommending trips to the emergency room, physicians can contribute to a more equitable health care delivery system.

120. Brennan, Troyen A. Silent Decisions: Limits of Consent and the Terminally Ill Patient. Law, Medicine & Health Care; Fall/Winter 1988; 16(3-4): 204-209.

Brennan argues that physicians have begun to limit care for individual decisionally incapacitated patients against the wishes of the patient's family. He argues that physicians should not be permitted to make unilateral, substituted decisions on behalf of such patients. Given the flaws of physician/patient communication and the failure of physicians properly to consider patient autonomy, the author posits that physicians are not equipped to make substituted decisions that primarily respect patient self-determination. Thus, he urges society to resist allowing physicians to overrule families with regard to limits on care for incapacitated patients. Brennan also discusses the relationship between patient autonomy and substituted judgment and the allocation of scarce resources. He argues that we must be careful to eliminate the potential that rationing decisions will be made silently by physicians in the absence of social consent.

121. Callahan, Daniel. What Kind of Life? The Limits of Medical Progress. New York: Simon and Schuster; 1990.

Philosopher Callahan provocatively proposes a radical reconceptualization and reprioritization of American values concerning health care. He argues that our insatiable thirst for medical progress exceeds both social resources and legitimate need, and that we ought to afford higher priority (i.e., money) to caring rather than curing within the health care system, and to satisfying other social needs besides health care. Much of the burden of the sort of health care rationing advocated by Callahan would fall on older persons, who now consume and benefit from many of the medical interventions that Callahan would curtail.

122. Callahan, Daniel. Rationing Health Care: Will It Be Necessary? Can It Be Done Without Age or Disability Discrimination? Issues in Law and Medicine; Winter 1989; 5(3): 353-366.

Health care rationing is necessary, according to Callahan, who proposes 'categorical standards' to do it: visible, objective, universal criteria that can be applied to all (or most) individuals and that do not require complex interpretation to be employed. The author attacks individual decisionmaking by the physician at the bedside as economically unworkable and leading to prejudiced, unjust results. Categorical standards would be more workable, successful, and fair than a continuation of our present highly individualistic policy. Using age as a categorical standard would not be discriminatory, since the elderly as a group are already singled out for special benefits under Medicare.

123. Callahan, Daniel. Old Age and New Policy. Journal of the American Medical Association; February 10, 1989; 261(6): 905-906.

Callahan defends his proposal that we set limits on life-extending, high technology care for the elderly. He urges society to move from a bias toward short-term, critical care medicine for the elderly to the provision of well-funded long-term care and all those other needs of the elderly that improve the quality of their day-to-day lives, though not necessarily extending those lives. He claims that his approach is less ageist than the current bias of the health care system.

124. Callahan, Daniel. Meeting Needs and Rationing Care. Law, Medicine & Health Care; Fall/Winter 1988; 16(3-4): 261-266.

Callahan argues that rationing scarce health care resources is inevitable, and that explicit or "hard" rationing as a matter of clear public policy is preferable to our current practice of silent or "soft" rationing based on economic and geographic circumstances. We need to set limits and to create the kind of psychological expectations necessary to do that. This would include fostering a new public understanding of aging and old age, as well as the proper goals of medicine concerning older persons.

125. Callahan, Daniel. Setting Limits: Medical Goals in an Aging Society.

New York: Simon and Schuster; 1987.

This bold book encourages society to formulate an alternative approach to thinking about old age, health care, and death. Callahan would exchange, quid pro quo, the present emphasis of medicine for the aging on life-extension with a new medical objective of comfort and support. Central to implementation of this social vision is Callahan's call for limitation of publicly funded (i.e., Medicare) acute medical treatment oriented primarily toward life-extension for persons who have already achieved a 'normal life span,' which he is generally prepared to peremptorily set for most purposes at about age eighty. In other words, this book advocates health care rationing according to chronological age.

126. Callahan, Daniel. Adequate Health Care and an Aging Society: Are They Morally Compatible? in Theme Issue on "The Aging Society": Daedalus: Journal of the American Academy of Arts and Sciences; Winter 1986; 115(1): 247-267.

Callahan describes three evolutionary stages in thinking about the ethics of formulating health policy in an aging society. In the first stage, we ask, given present social values, what options are available to control costs and thereby to preclude or forestall a signficant reduction in adequate health care for the elderly. At the second stage, we begin to move out of existing values and commitments and to ask what are or ought to be the moral foundations of health care programs and benefits for the elderly. The third stage raises difficult questions about whether we should interpret aging as a natural and inescapable biological process, to be accepted with grace and dignity, or as one more disease and corporeal derangement, to be fought with all the power that science and money can bring to bear.

127. Cassel, Christine K. Doctors and Allocation Decisions: A New Role in the New Medicare. Journal of Health Politics, Policy and Law; Fall 1985; 10(3): 549-563.

Dr. Cassel examines the cost containment pressures facing modern physicians who care for older, publicly-funded patients. She concludes that physicians may ethically (that is, consistent with their obligations to society and to the individual patient) take part in allocation decisions, as long as every person enjoys access to a minimum decent health care package, the physician does not have a direct financial stake in the treatment choice, and the system is a closed one in which tradeoffs in one area really provide gains in another.

128. Cassel, Christine K.; Purtilo, Ruth B. Justice and the Allocation of Health Care Resources. in: Cassel, Christine K.; Riesenberg, Donald E.; Sorenson, Leif B.; Walsh, John R., Editors. Geriatric Medicine. Second ed. New York: Springer-Verlag; 1990: Chapter 47, pp. 615-622.

This chapter discusses the subject of allocation of relatively scarce health care resources in light of distributive justice considerations, as such allocation would affect the elderly as major consumers of those resources. The authors consider the possibilities of allocation schemes based on merit, on societal contribution, and on need. They conclude that each of these approaches has ethical failings, but that the latter policy is the least objectionable to advocates for the elderly.

129. Childress, James F. Ensuring Care, Respect, and Fairness for the Elderly. Hastings Center Report; October 1984; 14(5): 27-31.

Arguing from principles of fairness and justice, Childress argues against lumping all older people together for health care rationing purposes. The heterogeneity of the elderly is ethically relevant. He also cautions that it is unfair and disrespectful to assume that, because of old age alone, people are incapable of making their own decisions about medical care. He urges further that we need a redirection of health priorities toward chronic care and prevention.

130. Churchill, Larry R. Should We Ration Health Care by Age? Journal of the American Geriatrics Society; July 1988; 36(7): 644-647.

Philosopher Churchill analyzes several of the most cogent arguments for rationing of health services by age, and finds those proposals singling out the elderly for special sacrifice morally untenable. He argues that such proposals should be taken seriously only if included in much larger schemes to make the health care system as a whole more fair and prudent.

131. Clark, Phillip G. The Social Allocation of Health Care Resources: Ethical Dilemmas in Age-Group Competition. Gerontologist; April 1985;

25(2): 119-125.

This article analyzes the specter of rivalry between age groups over the allocation of scarce health care resources. Clark discusses the ethical principle of justice as it should shape and guide decisions concerning the resolution of this competition, as well as the public policy implications of intergenerational dueling for public dollars.

132. Coile, Russell C., Jr. Technology and Ethics: Three Scenarios for the 1990s. Quality Review Bulletin; June 1990; 16(6): 202-208.

The author explores ethical issues raised by the growth of medical technology and its huge price tag, especially in light of an aging population. Futurist Coile predicts that in the coming decade an irresistible force (an aging population) will meet an immovable object (limited resources), and that the result will be an extension of the status quo, continuing America's love affair with medical technology despite its rising costs. Even with a high health inflation rate, Americans will find this investment affordable. Coile argues that politicians will find increased health spending hard to resist in the face of the strength of elderly voting power.

133. Daniels, Norman. Am I My Parents' Keeper? An Essay on Justice Between the Young and the Old. New York: Oxford University Press; 1988.

Philosopher Daniels seeks a principled way, rooted in Rawls' theory of justice, to guide decisions about how health care, as well as income support and other resources, should be allocated among different age groups. He uses a 'Prudential Lifespan' approach to discuss the allocation of medical services to the elderly, the adequacy of long term care, current cost containment efforts, and the fair distribution of income support over the lifespan and among generations. This is the first systematic theoretical discussion of the problems of distributive justice which arise between the young and the old.

134. Daniels, Norman. Just Health Care. New York: Cambridge University Press; 1985.

A philosopher explores the ethical dimensions of society's struggle with the allocation of medical resources among conflicting demands. The central argument, within which questions relating to treatment of the elderly are evaluated, is that health care has a crucial effect on equality of life opportunities, and that a principle guaranteeing equality of opportunity must underlie the distribution of health care services.

135. Daniels, Norman; Sabin, James E. Commentary: When Is Home Care Medically Necessary? Hastings Center Report; July/August 1991; 21(4): 37-38.

These authors argue, in the context of a hypothetical scenario, that a health maintenance organization should enforce its reasonable, consistent policy regarding medical necessity not merely as a matter of bureaucratic contractualism, but as a prerequisite for treating all patients in the plan equitably and a necessary bulwark against the corrosive deception and case-by-case gaming so pervasive in health care today.

136. Danis, Marion; Churchill, Larry R. Autonomy and the Common Weal. Hastings Center Report; January/February 1991; 21(1): 25-31.

The authors are bothered by the fact that much money is routinely expended in the United States to sustain an individual toward the end of life, at the same time that little or no health care coverage is provided to one-fifth of the American population. According to Danis and Churchill, when elderly individuals choose aggressive and expensive medical intervention at the end of life, their wishes conflict with the need to allocate resources in an efficient and equitable manner. What is required is an integrated moral framework that puts individual autonomy and social equity questions into focus simultaneously. This article proposes as such a framework the authors' concept of citizenship.

137. Dolenc, Danielle A.; Dougherty, Charles J. DRGs: The Counterrevolution in Financing Health Care. Hastings Center Report; June 1985; 15(3): 19-29.

These authors strongly criticize the movement to pay hospitals for caring for Medicare patients under a Prospective Payment System (PPS) computed according to Diagnosis Related Groups (DRGs). They submit that this cost containment strategy has negative ethical ramifications in terms of access to services, quality of services, and disincentives to develop and disseminate new medical technologies. They suggest modifications to tinker with the DRG system so that it does not disproportionately disadvantage the sickest and poorest groups of patients.

138. Dougherty, Charles J. Ethical Perspectives on Prospective Payment. Hastings Center Report; January/February 1989; 19(1): 5-11.

This article discusses the several and interrelated ethical issues raised by the prosepctive payment system (PPS) according to Diagnosis Related Groups (DRGs). Dougherty attacks DRGs from two ethical perspectives: utilitarian (the impact of the system, especially on the physician's role) and contractarian (the system's inconsistency with social justice regarding the problem of uncompensated care).

139. Dyer, Allen R. Should Doctors Cut Costs at the Bedside? Patients, Not Costs, Come First. Hastings Center Report; February 1986; 16(1): 5-7.

Dr. Dyer rejects thrusting on the physician at the bedside the role of society's agent in rationing care for the individual patient in order to reduce health care costs and conserve limited resources. Unilateral cost-cutting at the bedside would erode the foundations of the physician/patient relationship and compromise the quality of care. The author instead prefers for the physician to discuss the economic, as well as other, implications of care with the patient, so that informed joint decisions can be made.

140. Fahey, Charles J. Medical Ethics and Treatment of the Aged. in: Branstetter, Karen, Editor. The Maturing Society in the Maturing Health Care System. Columbus, OH: Ross Laboratories; 1984: 13-19.

A Jesuit philosopher reflects on the moral values shaping social policy toward the elderly, and particularly on the moral appropriateness of singling out the elderly for special social benefits. The moral obligations of the family to care for an aging member are discussed and compared to society's obligations vis-a-vis the care of older persons.

141. Fletcher, Joseph. The Moral Dimension in Clinical Decision Making. Pharos; 1987; 50(2): 2-4.

This article discusses the central ethical role and imperative of physicians as patient advocates in an era of cost containment and third-party reimbursement for health services.

142. Forrow, Lachlan. Commentary: When Is Home Care Medically Necessary? Hastings Center Report; July/August 1991; 21(4): 36-37.

The author argues that a broad interpretation of the concept of medical necessity is ethically mandated in the context of home care for older patients. Clinicians are obligated to force this broad interpretation on pre-paid or fee-for-service providers.

143. Greene, Vernon L. Human Capitalism and Intergenerational Justice. Gerontologist; December 1989; 29(6): 723-724.

This editorial rejects the idea of the necessity or appropriateness of rationing health benefits according to chronological age as a matter of generational equity or intergenerational justice.   Greene argues that the benefits that the elderly now receive are not a form of welfare, but rather what older persons deserve in return for the human capital that they have invested over the years in making society productive.   He calls on the different generations to work together in addressing resource scarcity problems.

144. Gritzer, Glenn; Arluke, Arnold. The Making of Rehabilitation. Berkeley: University of California Press; 1985.

This history of the development of rehabilitation medicine in the United States takes a market-oriented view of the field--that is, that the profession developed for materialistic reasons. The ethical themes suggested by this market model focus upon issues of professional responsibility and competency, conflict among team members, selection of patients for treatment, and allocation of scarce resources.

145. Hamner, James E. III; Jacobs, Barbara J., Editors. Life and Death Issues. Memphis: University of Tennessee Press; 1986.

This set of Proceedings from a 1985 conference contains essays on health care rationing, medical treatment at the end of life, and health care cost containment. Prominent philosophers and physicians are contributors.

146.   Homer, Paul; Holstein, Martha, Editors.   A Good Old Age?   The Paradox of Setting Limits. New York: Simon and Schuster; 1990.

This collection of essays responds to Callahan's proposal to limit medical care on the basis of chronological age from a variety of medical, legal, philosophical and economic perspectives. Over thirty authorities debate the consequences of medical progress in an aging society.

147. Jecker, Nancy S. Disenfranchising the Elderly from Life-Extending Medical Care. Public Affairs Quarterly; July 1988; 2(3): 51-68.

Jecker argues against age-based health care rationing schemes. Even if we accept the idea that there exists a "natural life span," we need not accept the claim that individuals who have passed that marker have no right to government-supported life-extending medical services. Also, the author wants us to be skeptical about the prospect of achieving a consensus concerning ideal old age and death. If age-based rationing is to be acceptable morally, it must be founded on some theory other than a natural life span.

148. Jecker, Nancy S. Towards a Theory of Age-Group Justice. Journal of Medicine and Philosophy; 1989; 14: 655-676.

Philosopher Jecker examines the question of intergenerational equity and the distribution of scarce medical resources. She launches a concentrated attack on philosopher Norman Daniels' "prudential lifespan" approach to the allocation among age-group question.   Jecker points out the inherent difficulties in crafting a just age-group allocation strategy, but does not offer a plan of her own for overcoming those problems.

149. Jecker, Nancy S.; Pearlman, Robert A. Ethical Constraints on Rationing Medical Care by Age. Journal of the American Geriatrics Society; November 1989; 37(11): 1067-1075.

This article supports the position of the American Geriatrics Society Public Policy Committee that chronological age should not be used as the sole, arbitrary criterion for rationing health care resources. The authors examine and reject on ethical grounds current proposals for age-based rationing. Instead, they posit special social duties toward the elderly that protect them against automatic exclusion.

150. Jonsen, Albert R. Bentham in a Box: Technology Assessment and Health Care Allocation. Law, Medicine & Health Care; September 1986; 14(3-4): 172-174.

Philosopher Jonsen criticizes current ways of thinking about the problem of resource allocation as too confined. He believes that we are boxed in on this subject by attempts to determine cost-effectiveness through the process of technology assessment coming into conflict directly with a felt imperative to rescue endangered life at any price. If we remain conceptually confined between these two forces, the author believes that it will be difficult to allocate resources justly.

151. Kalb, Paul E.; Miller, David H. Utilization Strategies for Intensive Care Units. Journal of the American Medical Association; April 28, 1989; 261(16): 2389-2395.

Rationing of intensive care services in the United States according to subjective, unspoken criteria that, among other things, discriminates against the elderly, occurs all the time. Looking at the individual hospital or ICU level, these authors examine the elements of fair rationing (equality, equity, utilitarianism, and distribution according to need), present the arguments in favor of rationing, and propose the outline of a model rationing system. They then marshal the arguments against rationing potentially beneficial care, discuss ways in which it can be avoided, and provide empirical data to support this approach.

152. Kane, Robert L.; Kane, Rosalie A. The Impact of Long-Term-Care Financing on Personal Autonomy. Generations; 1990; 14(Supplement): 86-89.

This article describes how financing arrangements for nursing homes and home care affect the personal autonomy of consumers for reasons that have nothing to do with efforts to minimize the public price. This is because the payor for services is in a position to impose certain rules. When rules are made by public officials who have multiple goals, they may include provisions for standards of quality, equitable distribution of benefits, fair reimbursement, ease of administration, clear accountability, development of an agency infrastructure, and personnel development. As these goals become operational, the policies that accompany the flow of money can interfere with the personal autonomy of clients.

153. Kapp, Marshall B. Rationing Health Care: Will It Be Necessary? Can It Be Done Without Age or Disability Discrimination? Issues in Law and Medicine; Winter 1989; 5(3): 337-351.

This article argues that there are strategies for reducing the severity of the health care financing problem (for example, eliminating use of futile, non-beneficial medical interventions), but ultimately some health care must be rationed. It examines Callahan's call for explicit, age-based rationing and criticizes it on political (e.g., exacerbating intergenerational antagonism), legal (due process, equal protection, privacy, freedom of contract), and ethical (e.g., devaluing the elderly, injuring physician/patient relationship, reneging on promises, justice) grounds. As an alternative to age-based rationing, Kapp endorses a comprehensive, universal national health insurance program with tight cost controls. He also suggests that financially capable elders pay their fair share for health care.

154. Kapp, Marshall B. Health Care Tradeoffs Based on Age: Ethically Confronting the 'R' Word. Pharos of Alpha Omega Alpha; Summer 1989; 52(3): 2-7.

The author argues that we cannot avoid confronting the issue of health care rationing generally, and rationing by age particularly. Societal tradeoffs are inevitable. The article examines proposals by Callahan, Daniels, and Veatch for age-based rationing. Kapp must react to this debate by explicit policymaking (not policymaking by default) and by keeping policymaking in the public (i.e., accountable) sector. Bedside rationing by individual physicians is less desirable ethically than social responsibility for setting treatment parameters, although physicians would still be on the 'moral hook' to apply societal guidelines to specific patients. See also Letter to the Editor and Response, at Pharos, Volume 52, Number 4, page 30 (Fall 1989).

155. Kapp, Marshall B. Hospital Reimbursement by Diagnosis-Related Groups: Legal and Ethical Implications for Nursing Homes. Journal of

Long-Term Care Administration; Fall 1986; 14(3): 20-26.

This article examines the current ethical and legal challenges to nursing homes caused by receiving patients who are being discharged from acute care hospitals "sicker and quicker" because of cost containment pressures. Nursing homes now need to provide more sub-acute care to patients, maintaining acceptable professional standards, while operating within severe financial constraints themselves.

156. Kapp, Marshall B. Legal and Ethical Standards in Geriatric Medicine. Journal of the American Geriatrics Society; March 1985; 33(3): 179-183.

This article discusses the older person's ethical and legal right to access to beneficial medical services, and on the extent and limits of the physician's corresponding duties to assist the patient to obtain such access. The impact of cost containment strategies on the fulfillment of these obligations is noted.

157. Kapp, Marshall B. Legal and Ethical Implications of Health Care Reimbursement by Diagnosis Related Groups. Law, Medicine & Health Care; December 1984; 12(6): 245-253.

This article speculates on the ethical and legal ramifications of the DRG system of attempting to contain Medicare costs for the hospitalized elderly. The proper role of physicians as participants in a societal health care rationing process for older patients is discussed. Possible implications for the standard of care available to the elderly are also mentioned.

158. Kilner, John F. Who Lives? Who Dies? Ethical Criteria in Patient Selection. New Haven, CT: Yale University Press; 1990.

The author examines sixteen criteria for deciding ethically which patients should receive medical treatment in a time of scarcity. Among other things, he discusses the place of random selection, the role of patients' wishes, the relevance of quality of life, and whether selection criteria should be different when the resources involved are experimental. Case studies illustrate how health professionals talk about rationing criteria.

159. Lamm, Richard D. Critical Decisions in Medical Care: Birth to Death. Southern Medical Journal; July 1989; 82(7): 822-824.

From a politician's perspective, a former Colorado governor examines the ethical implications of a health care system where "the genius of American medicine has simply outstripped our ability to pay." He argues that the cumulative effect of all of the individual ethical decisions made by physicians, patients, and families has made for unethical public policy. Lamm blames much of the difficulty in confronting squarely the ethical problem of equitable distribution of health resources on the political power of the elderly lobby.

160. Lamm, Richard D. Misallocating Health Care and Societal Resources. Notre Dame Journal of Law, Ethics & Public Policy; 1988; 3(2): 241-248.

A former Colorado governor argues that, in an age of infinite needs and finite resources, society has no moral choice but to rearrange health care priorities to give less preference to high technology interventions likely to benefit a relatively small number and greater weight to preventive public health measures. These shifted priorities might work against the interests of individual older patients.

161. LaPuma, John; Cassel, Christine K.; Humphrey, Holly. Ethics, Economics, and Endocarditis: The Physician's Role in Resource Allocation. Archives of Internal Medicine; August 1988; 148(8): 1809-1811.

Using a case example, the physician authors suggest how clinicians might use principles of medical ethics to allocate scarce resources in clinical situations. They argue that, ideally, resource allocation decisions ought to be made as social policy choices, in health care institutions and legislatures, while physicians continue to advocate for individual patients. This article suggests how physicians might participate in the process of institutional allocation of scarce resources.

162. Lee, Robert G.; Miller, Frances H. The Doctor's Changing Role in Allocating U.S. and British Medical Services. Law, Medicine & Health Care; Spring/Summer 1990; 18(1-2): 69-76.

This article examines evolution of the British and American physician's role in filtering clinical need from patient demand for health services, and in setting relative priorities among patient needs. It then raises questions about the significance of this change in roles for the nature of the physician-patient relationship.

163. Levinsky, Norman G. Health Care for Veterans: The Limits of Obligation. Hastings Center Report; August 1986; 16(4): 10-14.

Dr. Levinsky argues that society owes no special moral obligation to provide free health care to military veterans for nonservice-connected medical problems. Instead, society's moral responsibilities regarding access to health services ought to apply to all persons, regardless of veteran status.

164. Luce, John M. Improving the Quality and Utililization of Critical Care. Quality Review Bulletin; February 1991; 17(2): 42-47.

Although nominally eschewing the use of formal rationing policies, Dr. Luce advocates the development of admission and discharge policies to guide physicians during periods of low critical care bed availability. He urges greater leadership roles for critical care unit directors, while recognizing that such a heightened role raises ethical and legal issues about the autonomy of both patients and physicians.

165. Mariner, Wendy K. Diagnosis Related Groups: Evading Social Responsibility? Law, Medicine & Health Care; December 1984; 12(6): 243-244.

Mariner argues that the federal government's adoption of a Prospective Payment System (PPS) computed according to Diagnosis Related Groups (DRGs) for hospital reimbursement under Medicare improperly and unethically compels physicians to act as bedside rationers of health care for their older patients. She suggests that allocation of resources, if necessary, should be done at the societal level instead.

166. Moody, Harry R. Allocation, Yes; Age-Based Rationing, No. in: Binstock, Robert H.; Post, Stephen G., Editors. Too Old for Health Care? Controversies in Medicine, Law, Economics, and Ethics. Glenview, IL: Scott Foresman & Company; 1990: Chapter 8.

Philosopher Moody accepts, in theory, Daniel Callahan's concept of a regulative ideal of a natural life course as a standard for allocating health care resources. Moody departs from Callahan, however, over the pragmatic principles and political actions to be drawn from that regulative ideal. In this chapter, Moody tries to bridge the gap between philosophical theory and medical and political practice regarding age-based health care rationing.

167. Moody, Harry R. Rationing Medical Resources on Grounds of Age: A Senario for the Future? Generations; Winter 1985; 10(2): 43-44.

Moody looks at the growing debate about explicit rationing of health care services based on the patient's age, and suggests that denial of potentially beneficial care on this basis may already go on silently more than we would like to admit. He points to the English model, in which age-based decisions masquerade in the language of medical indications and quality of life, and surmises the extension of this practice to the United States.

168. Morreim, E. Haavi. Cost Containment: Challenging Fidelity and Justice. Hastings Center Report; December 1988; 18(6): 20-25.

The federal government's movement in the early 1980s to reimbursement of hospitals under Medicare according to a Prospective Payment System (PPS) based on Diagnosis Related Groups (DRGs) gave strong impetus to the cost containment mood that has characterized the American health care industry in the past decade and a half. Philosopher Morreim explores some of the ethical problems accompanying the cost containment initiative in health care, especially challenges to the fiduciary nature of the physician/patient relationship (including the obligation of fidelity or loyalty) and questions of justice arising from hard resource distribution choices.

169. Morreim, E. Haavi. Gaming the System: Dodging the Rules, Ruling the Dodgers. Archives of Internal Medicine; March 1991; 151(3): 443-447.

This article comments on the growing practice of physicians who "game" or "fudge" the reimbursement system to try to obtain more health care resources for their individual patients. Philosopher Morreim acknowledges the temptation of this practice in light of current cost containment developments, but argues that such gaming is morally and medically hazardous by potentially injuring patients and others, offending the principle of honesty, and violating basic precepts of contractual and distributive justice. In fact, the author suggests, there usually are better alternatives available to the physician than going around the system while pretending to play by the stated rules.

170. Morreim, E. Haavi. Cost Constraints As a Malpractice Defense. Hastings Center Report; February/March 1988; 18(1): 5-10.

Philosopher Morreim argues that, as a matter of ethics and public policy, legal standards of care in medical malpractice cases may need to be altered--that is, made less demanding--to account for the strong cost containment pressures that characterize the modern health care arena. She examines the moral implications (e.g., the balance of fiduciary and fiscal obligations) of a shift in legally enforceable standards.

171. Morreim, E. Haavi. The MD and the DRG. Hastings Center Report; June 1985; 15(3): 30-31.

Philosopher Morreim argues against the ethical propriety of individual physicians making bedside treatment decisions for particular patients on the basis of economic considerations. However, as a matter of social responsibility, she urges the medical profession to collectively review and revise, taking financial aspects into account, informal treatment protocols which help set the parameters within which individual medical decision making takes place.

172. Orona, Celia J. Moral Aspects of Giving Care. Generations; Fall 1989; 13(4): 60-62.

This article addresses the process of fulfilling a moral commitment to provide care to a partner who has AIDS dementia or Alzheimer's disease. The family or friend caregiver in either situation personifies the best of social values and also the complexity of a very difficult and widespread situation.

173. Powderly, Kathleen E.; Smith, Elaine. The Impact of DRGs on Health Care Workers and Their Clients. Hastings Center Report; January/February 1989; 19(1): 16-18.

The authors are bothered that the advent of paying hospitals for Medicare patients under a Diagnosis Related Group (DRG) system has forced a reversal of professional priorities that places cost containment first, ahead of advocacy for the patient. This raises a number of ethical dilemmas for providers (the main concern here is with nurses and social workers) and patients, in terms of changes from the traditional roles and relationships.

174. President's Commission for the Study of Ethical Problems in Medicine and Biomedical and Behavioral Research. Securing Access to Health Care: A Report on the Ethical Implications of Differences in the Availability of Health Services. Washington, DC: U.S. Government Printing Office; March 1983.

This report looks comprehensively at the ethical issues raised by the existence of limited health resources and the uneven distribution of those resources across the population. Rights and obligations on the part of both individuals and society are discussed, as are various public policy strategies for attempting to deal with the equity issue.

175. Relman, Arnold S. The Trouble With Rationing. New England Journal of Medicine; September 27, 1990; 323(13): 911-913.

Editor Relman argues that explicit rationing of health resources is not necessary, nor would it be likely to work without major changes in the American health care system. Furthermore, a fair and workable rationing plan would be virtually impossible to design. Our cost crisis, and the limitations on access that result from high costs, stem from an inherently inflationary and wasteful health care delivery system. Rationing is not likely to be successful in controlling costs unless we deal with the basic structural problems.

176. Sage, William M.; Hurst, Carolyn R.; Silverman, James F.; Bortz, Walter M. Intensive Care for the Elderly: Outcome of Elective and Nonelective Admissions. Journal of the American Geriatrics Society; April 1987; 35(4): 312-318.

This study found that a patient's acute, and to an even larger extent chronic, health are better predictors of long-term survival than age. Age alone does not constitute a barrier to survival or functional recovery and many elderly intensive care patients continue to lead rewarding and productive lives. Therefore, it is ethically objectionable to ration intensive care resources solely on the basis of chronological age.

177. Schiedermayer, David L.; LaPuma, John; Miles, Steven H. Ethics Consultation Masking Economic Dilemmas in Patient Care. Archives of Internal Medicine; June 1989; 149(6): 1303-1305.

The authors use cases from their ethics consultation service (including some involving older patients) to note the growing number of instances in which they are asked for ethical advice in situations really exacerbated by financial constraints or conflicts. Some of these consultations arise when medical interventions conflict with private or third-party resources available to finance treatment. Other considerations arise when physicians themselves are financially affected by their decision to provide medically indicated therapy. Still others occur when physicians wish to save society money by withholding indicated treatment from certain patients.

178. Schneider, Edward L. Options to Control the Rising Health Care Costs of Older Americans. Journal of the American Medical Association; February 10, 1989; 261(6): 907-908.

Dr. Schneider argues against proposals to ration health care according to the patient's chronological age. Instead, he urges that this is a step backwards that removes families, affected individuals, and their physicians from the decisionmaking process. Any decision to withhold care should be made based on other criteria, such as the patient's prognosis and the desires of the patient and family. Using age alone as a criterion for decisionmaking wrongly implies that older persons make up a homogeneous group.

179. Siegler, Mark. Should Age Be a Criterion in Health Care? Hastings Center Report; October 1984; 14(5): 24-27.

Siegler detects a disturbing shift in the way medical treatment decisions are made about elderly patients. Traditionally, medical indications and the patient's preferences weighed most heavily. In the future, in what the author terms the Age of Bureaucratic Parsimony, the good of the patient will have to be weighed against other private and social goods and needs. The article predicts that strategies of cost containment will have dire consequences for the elderly. If rationing is necessary, Siegler urges, it should be begun not with the elderly but with patients who are best able to articulate on their own behalf.

180. Silver, Jessica D. From Baby Doe to Grandpa Doe: The Impact of the Federal Age Discrimination Act on the Hidden Rationing of Medical Care. Catholic University Law Review; 1988; 37: 993-1072.

The author reviews the circumstances that have led to proposals for hidden health care rationing and suggests the impact such a scheme could have on older persons. She then examines the federal Age Discrimination Act and its likely impact on the use of age as a rationing criteria. Silver is optimistic that the mere possibility of legal challenge will expose the medical decisionmaking process and the serious issues surrounding the rationing of medical care to public scrutiny.

181. Smeeding, Timothy M., Editor. Should Medical Care be Rationed by Age? Totowa, NJ: Rowman and Littlefield; 1987.

This collection of essays presents a multidisciplinary discussion of critical issues surrounding the question of rationing health care by chronological age. Topics covered include the implications of demographic change for health care costs, the ethics of prolonging life artificially, the British system of implicit rationing, and criteria for selecting which patients should receive treatment. Directions for further study on the topic of age-based health care rationing are identified.

182. Somerville, Margaret A. Should the Grandparents Die?: Allocation of Medical Resources with an Aging Population. Law, Medicine & Health Care; September 1986; 14(3-4): 158-163.

Somerville discusses the ethical and public policy implications of rationing potentially beneficial health care on the basis of age in order to conserve and re-direct scarce resources. If such rationing must be done, the author suggests ways that it might be accomplished with the least degree of unfairness. She distinguishes between allocation decisions made at the individual level from those made by institutions and governments.

183. Sommers, Christina H. Once a Soldier, Always a Dependent. Hastings Center Report; August 1986; 16(4): 15-17.

Philosopher Sommers contends that society is ethically obligated to provide free medical care to military veterans without limit. The basis for this responsibility/entitlement is not utilitarian, but rather the quasi-familial relationship that is formed between a soldier and the country that he or she serves.

184. Spicker, Stuart F., Guest Editor. Prospective Payment: DRGs and Ethics. Journal of Medicine and Philosophy; May 1987; 12(2).

The contributors to this symposium discuss the ethical, as well as the economic, implications of Prospective Payment Systems (PPSs) such as Diagnosis Related Groups (DRGs), including notions of economic incentives in the physician/patient relationship, conceptions of justive formulated to assess DRGs, and the ethics of a severity of illness (SI) index for fine-tuning PPS/DRG reimbursement.

185. Thomasma, David C. Moving the Aged Into the House of the Dead: A Critique of Ageist Social Policy. Journal of the American Geriatrics Society; February 1989; 37(2): 169-172.

The author severely criticizes recent proposals to ration health care resources according to the chronological age of the patient. Serious difficulties with these proposals include inequities of access, a lack of respect for the aged and gratitude for what they have contributed, the creation of institutional dumping grounds for the elderly, unjust decisionmaking for incompetent persons, and cutting off care for many elderly persons who could benefit from it.

186. Thornton, James E.; Winkler, Earl R., Editors. Ethics and Aging: The Right to Live, The Right to Die. Vancouver, B.C., Canada: University of British Columbia Press; 1988.

This collection of essays by Canadian philosophers, psychologists, and gerontologists address the ethical dimensions of public policy affecting the elderly: the place and claims--i.e., the status, roles, and welfare--of the elderly in society. The book deals with questions of social justice and resource allocation in health care. The authors debate concerns about respective responsibilities and rights, including the standard of care owed, by and to the elderly.

187. Veatch, Robert M. DRGs and the Ethical Reallocation of Resources. Hastings Center Report; June 1986; 16(3): 32-33.

To allocate limited health resources under a prospective payment system (PPS) based on Diagnosis Related Groups (DRGs), we need a medical ethics that focuses less exclusively on individual autonomy and more on social principles of beneficence and distributive justice. If rationing of beneficial care must occur, weighting decisions should be made at a level other than the specific physician at the bedside.

188. Veatch, Robert M. Justice and the Economics of Terminal Illness. Hastings Center Report; August/September 1988; 18(4): 34-40.

Philosopher Veatch sets forth an egalitarian theory of justice over a lifetime that permits society to exclude provision of (i.e., to ration) certain kinds of medical care based on terminal illness or chronological age. For Veatch, an individual's moral claim to health care, even if it is likely to be beneficial, diminishes in direct proportion to one's age. Put differently, when one is old, he has already had his opportunities, and it is time to give younger persons the same chances that the older person enjoyed in his own youth.

189. Veatch, Robert M. Physicians and Cost Containment. Jurimetrics Journal; Summer 1990; 30:461-482.

An ethicist discusses the possible roles for physicians, health care administrators, and laypersons in allocating scarce health care resources in an equitable fashion. Veatch concludes that societal mechanisms for rationing care are preferable to individual, ad hoc bedside decisions by physicians that would attempt to balance costs against the welfare of patients.

190. Webster, James R.; Berdes, Celia. Ethics and Economic Realities: Goals and Strategies for Care Toward the End of Life. Archives of Internal Medicine; September 1990; 150(9): 1795-1797.

The authors begin by examining the economic realities of providing medical care to the critically and chronically ill elderly in the contemporary United States. In light of the economic environment, they then address (1) broad questions of setting priorities within health care consistent with distributive justice and equity and (2) specific strategies (principally a reorientation of the physician/patient relationship to include enhanced education and negotiation) that physicians and other health professionals can use effectively to benefit their patients.

191. Weil, Max H.; Weil, Carol J.; Rackow, Eric C. Guide to Ethical Decision-Making for the Critically Ill: The Three R's and Q.C. Critical Care Medicine; June 1988; 16(6): 636641.

These authors propose an ethical model for medical decision making in critical care situations that begins at the bedside with considerations of whether a proposed intervention is (a) rational, (b) redeeming, and (c) respectful. When the ethical issues cannot be resolved successfully at this first tier, the physician should proceed to questions about quality of life and cost.   In assessing these factors, the physician may need the input of experts from several other disciplines.

192. Welch, H. Gilbert. Comparing Apples and Oranges: Does Cost-Effectiveness Analysis Deal Fairly With the Old and Young? Gerontologist; June 1991; 31(3): 332-336.

The author considers the proper effect of age on the outcome of cost-effectiveness analysis (CEA), which is a process that policymakers are paying attention to in terms of making decisions about the allocation of resources.   Welch argues that CEA is not strictly objective, but rather inevitably involves a value judgment about the worth of therapies to persons of different ages.   CEA cannot obviate the need for these value judgments, and the decision about the appropriate effect of age should not be relegated to technical considerations such as the choice of a discount rate.

4

Caregiving

193. Ambrogi, Donna M. Nursing Home Admissions: Problematic Process and Agreements. Generations; 1990; 14(Supplement): 72-74.

The author analyzes the nursing home admission process, including the written admission agreement or contract, in terms of the impact on the new resident's autonomy. She offers policy recommendations for enhancing the positive role of admission agreements and for decreasing their negative effects on autonomy.

194. Ambrogi, Donna M.; Leonard, Frances. The Impact of Nursing Home Admission Agreements on Resident Autonomy. Gerontologist; June 1988; 28(Supplement): 82-89.

This studied identified the way in which nursing home admission contracts in California routinely contained clauses that impaired resident autonomy regarding health care decisions and other personal choices, due process or grievance procedures, and informed financial choices. Recommendations for reform, many of which have been adopted in California and elsewhere, and their ramifications for personal autonomy are made.

195. Arras, John D. A Philosopher's View. Generations; Spring 1987; 11(4): 65-66.

This article presents a philosopher's perspective on the subject of involuntary placement of elderly persons in nursing homes. While caregivers who disagree with a patient's decision to refuse institutional placement should try to change the patient's mind if safety considerations point toward nursing home care, the author argues that, where disagreement persists, there ought to be a very strong presumption in favor of the patient's autonomy.

196. Callahan, Daniel. What Do Children Owe Elderly Parents? Hastings Center Report; April 1985; 15(2): 32-37.

Philosopher Callahan explores the moral nature of the parent/child relationship. He asks particularly the extent to which we ought to expect children to sacrifice in order to honor their parents. This essay looks at the changing status of the elderly in the United States, what the law requires in terms of family obligations, the notion of parents as friends, and the formidable power of dependence to morally coerce responsibility by children. Callahan distinguishes between physical and financial assistance between the generations.

197. Clark, Phillip G. Autonomy, Personal Empowerment, and Quality of Life in Long-Term Care. Journal of Applied Gerontology; September 1988; 7(3): 279-297.

Philosopher Clark analyzes the dialectic between dependence and autonomy in advancing age, particularly when long term care services may be required to support the individual's personal needs. The need for assistance, for relying on others to meet one's basic functional requirements, does not connote a devaluation of the worth of the individual. What is required of service providers is a sensitivity to how each person strikes the balance between dependence and independence in his or her own life.

198. Cohler, Bertram J. Autonomy and Interdependence in the Family of Adulthood: A Psychological Perspective. Gerontologist; February 1983; 23(1): 33-39.

This article examines the family relationships of older persons from a psychological viewpoint, and asserts that the most important contribution of family ties to personal adjustment across the second half of life may well be support of individual autonomy rather than the interdependence so important in fostering personal adjustment earlier in adulthood.

199. Collopy, Bart; Boyle, Philip; Jennings, Bruce. New Directions in Nursing Home Ethics. Hastings Center Report; March-April 1991; 21(2): Supplement 1-16.

This report of a two-year project on nursing home ethics comprehensively surveys the ethically-relevant characteristics and problems that are unique to American long term care institutions. The authors explore the relationship between extensive regulation of the nursing home industry and the provision of good ethical care. They also probe how notions based on acute care, particularly individualistic conceptions of autonomy and interests, can be modified so that they resonate more fully with the predicaments of nursing home residents, caregivers, and family members.

200. Collopy, Bart; Dubler, Nancy N.; Zuckerman, Connie. The Ethics of Home Care: Autonomy and Accommodation. Hastings Center Report; March/April 1990; 20(2): Supplement 1-16.

This study explores the nature of home care, tracking issues of both client and caregiver autonomy. The authors' goal is to suggest a model of autonomy that recognizes the value of accommodation between moral agents in the highly cooperative tasks and tightly constrained conditions that define home care. They also indicate where the acute care model of autonomy does not serve the distinctive elements of home care.

201. Daniels, Norman. Family Responsibility Initiatives and Justice Between Age Groups. Law, Medicine & Health Care; September 1985; 13(4): 153-159.

Philosopher Daniels discusses the scope and limits of filial moral obligations regarding the care of older parents. He argues that attempts to enforce family obligations to provide long term care, through enactment of state family responsibility laws, should not be a feature of public policy. His theory of a just distribution of resources among age groups calls for a social obligation to design models that coordinate family and public support for long term care of the elderly.

202. Dubler, Nancy N. Autonomy and Accommodation: Mediating Individual Choice in the Home Setting. Generations; 1990; 14(Supplement): 29-31.

In home care, many individuals other than the patient possess moral interests or claims that demand respect. All of these parties and their various interests must be accounted for in fashioning an ethically acceptable and practically feasible homecare plan. The author explains how, in this process, the concept the concept of accommodation rather than the solitary principle of autonomy should determine an ethically appropriate arrangement.

203. Dubler, Nancy N. Refusals of Medical Care in the Home Setting. Law, Medicine & Health Care; Fall 1990; 18(3): 227-233.

Using a case example, this article explores the ethical questions that arise when an older person refuses medical care within the home health setting. Dubler sets out a suggested standard for respecting the refusal of homecare clients that tries to balance considerations of autonomy and beneficence.

204. Dubler, Nancy N. Improving the Discharge Planning Process: Distinguishing Between Coercion and Choice. Gerontologist; June 1988; 28(Supplement): 76-81.

This study combined the perspectives of anthropologic observation and philosophical and legal analysis to examine an array of ethical issues arising within the process of discharge planning for older patients leaving an acute care hospital. Practice and policy advice is given for resolving the ethical tensions in a manner that respects and supports the patient's autonomous preferences.

205. DuBois, Monica M. Community-Based Home Care Programs Are Not for Everyone--Yet. Caring; July 1990; 9(7): 24-28.

Using case examples, this article describes tensions that may arise in the process of case management and the provision of home care services for frail older persons, where patient preferences, considerations of safety, resource limitations, and perceived liability risks pull in different directions. The question of the client's mental capacity to make decisions is often an issue of significant ethical concern without an easy means of resolution.

206. Forrow, Lachlan. Commentary: When Is Home Care Medically

Necessary? Hastings Center Report; July/August 1991; 21(4): 36-37.

The author argues that a broad interpretation of the concept of medical necessity is ethically mandated in the context of home care for older patients. Clinicians are obligated to force this broad interpretation on pre-paid or fee-for-service providers.

207. Gibson, Joan M.; Nathanson, Paul S. Medical Treatment Guardians: When Someone Else Must Decide. Generations; 1990; 14(Supplement): 43-46.

This article describes a New Mexico demonstration project in which volunteers were trained and utilized as surrogate medical decision makers for older hospitalized patients without available family and friends. The volunteers faced ethical challenges as they sought to reconstruct the patient's "voice" so that decisions could be made that were most consistent with the patient's own authentic values.

208. Haddad, Amy M.; Kapp, Marshall B. Ethical and Legal Issues in Home Health Care. Norwalk, CT: Appleton & Lange; 1991.

Through both didactic presentation and case history analysis, this text analyzes ethical, as well as legal dilemmas, frequently encountered by home health agencies and their professional and paraprofessional personnel. The subject matter includes both the agency/client relationship and the ethical issues that arise in the course of an agency fulfilling its functions as a business and an employer.

209. Hiller, Marc D.; Sugarman, David B. Value Judgments in Long-Term Care: A Survey of NHAs. Journal of Long-Term Care Administration; Winter 1988; 16(4): 5-12.

This article describes a survey of licensed nursing home administrators (NHAs) conducted to examine the influence of ethical principles and personal values on decision making in long term care facilities. The first objective of the study was to explore the question of who (including the NHA) should be involved in various decisions concerning managerial and clinical issues in nursing homes. The second objective was to investigate the substantive principle of distributive justice employed by NHAs in making decisions, utilizing resident admissions as a model where perceptions of individual and social justice influence NHA choices. The article includes an overview of some literature on ethics and long term health care administration.

210. Hogstel, Mildred O.; Gaul, Alice L. Safety or Autonomy: An Ethical Issue for Clinical Gerontological Nurses. Journal of Gerontological Nursing; 1991; 17(3): 6-11.

This article discusses the ethical dilemma that arises for gerontological nurses when an older person residing in the community insists that he or she is capable of continued independence in his or her own home, but the older person's family insists that the environment is unsafe and that their loved one should be placed in an institution for his or her own protection. The nurse in this situation must resolve the apparent tension between the individual's autonomy, on one hand, and the principles of beneficence (helping) and nonmaleficence (doing no harm), on the other.

211. Iris, Madelyn A. Threats to Autonomy in Guardianship Decision Making. Generations; 1990; 14(Supplement): 39-41.

Iris maintains that guardianship is the form of legal protection that potentially is most intrusive to the autonomy of the individual for whom the guardianship is imposed. She examines some of the competing value systems and motivations influencing the guardianship decisionmaking process.

212. Iris, Madelyn A. Guardianship and the Elderly: A Multi-Perspective View of the Decisionmaking Process. Gerontologist; June 1988; 28(Supplement): 39-45.

An ethnographer studied four modes of decisionmaking for older persons under a guardianship: family, attorneys, physicians, and judges. Iris found that social attitudes and beliefs about aging significantly affect how ethical tensions are resolved within the guardianship decisionmaking process.

213. Kane, Rosalie A.; Caplan, Arthur L., Editors. Everyday Ethics: Resolving Dilemmas in Nursing Home Life. New York: Springer Publishing Company; 1990.

This series of essays by experts in ethics, law, and gerontology consists of commentaries to hypothetical cases presenting mundane but significant ethical questions arising within institutional long term care settings.   Questions concerning the delicate balancing of moral principles in the context of decisionmaking about activities such as dressing, eating, toileting, and sleeping are analyzed.   These are questions that generally do not concern courts or regulators, but that exert a major impact on the quality of life for nursing home residents, their families, and facility staff.

214. Kapp, Marshall B. Forcing Services on At-Risk Older Adults: When Doing Good Is Not So Good. Social Work in Health Care; 1988; 13(4): 1-13.

This article examines the natural ethical tensions between autonomy and beneficence when a question arises about whether protective services should be imposed on an older, at-risk individual over her objection. The respective rights and responsibilities of older person and social service providers in this relationship are analyzed.

215. Loewy, Erich H. Social Contract, Communities and Guardians. Journal of Elder Abuse and Neglect; 1990; 2(3/4): 123-143.

This article examines the way that different notions of social contract and community change the way in which we look at the obligations guardians have toward their wards. The author discusses the consequences for guardians of an autonomy-based (minimalist) versus a beneficence-based (non-minimalist) ethic for the elderly and others at risk.

216. Loewy, Erich H. Decisions to Leave Home: What Will the Neighbors Say? Journal of the American Geriatrics Society; December 1988; 36(12): 1143-1146.

The author examines two issues that arise when old, frail persons are cared for in their homes rather than in institutions. First, he looks at the problem of a sudden emergency which often prompts the family to call for assistance in almost a reflexive manner, and which then may result in hospital admission and all its sequelae. Second, he discusses the situation of an intercurrent condition that may require institutional treatment for either the patient's comfort or because of the inability of the family to cope. Dr. Loewy suggests a supportive approach to resolving such circumstances, involving the community as well as the patient, family, and health providers.

217. Lynn, Joanne. Ethical Issues in Caring for Elderly Residents of Nursing Homes. Primary Care; June 1986; 13(2): 295-306.

This article outlines four ethical areas relevant to nursing home residents: informed consent, with special attention to voluntariness and competence; decisions affecting admission to a nursing home or hospital; decisions affecting time or mode of dying; and general problems with financing and rationing of care. Guidance is provided to the primary care physician for managing these issues.

218. May, William F. Who Cares for the Elderly? Hastings Center Report; December 1982; 12(6): 31-37.

Philosopher May examines the philosophical underpinnings of American patterns of caring for older persons today. Current strategies he identifies in caring for the aging are reliance on families, public (financial) support so that older persons can participate in the marketplace, and placement in total institutions. He is especially critical of institutionalization, calling nursing homes a form of "geriatric barracks." He urges as an alternative to the huge bureaucracy that organizes gerontological professionals the development of a voluntary community that mobilizes outsiders.

219. Meier, Diane E.; Cassel, Christine K. Nursing Home Placement and the Demented Patient: A Case Presentation and Ethical Analysis. Annals of Internal Medicine; January 1986; 104(1): 98-105.

Centered around a case report, these geriatricians explore the moral perspectives and obligations of the patient, family, and health professionals in making decisions about the placement of a demented patient. A methodology for identifying and attempting various alternatives, from less to more restrictive of personal autonomy, is developed.

220. Moody, Harry R. Ethical Dilemmas in Nursing Home Placement. Generations; Summer 1987; 11(4): 16-23.

Philosopher Moody examines and explicates the distinctive ethical dilemmas involved in the involuntary placement of the frail elderly in nursing homes. He argues that the legal due process model, which would equate nursing home placement with involuntary civil commitment to a mental institution, is inadequate to deal with the ethical subtleties present. He proposes instead a new type of paternalism that is unencumbered by ideological presuppositions about the nature of nursing home care.

221. Moss, Robert J.; LaPuma, John. The Ethics of Mechanical Restraints. Hastings Center Report; January/February 1991; 21(1): 22-25.

The authors identify and analyze the ethical considerations posed for health care professionals when they consider using mechanical (physical) restraints in the care of elderly patients. The authors argue that, since mechanical restraints pose known medical risk and there is insufficient validation of both their safety and efficacy, their use in clinical practice should be understood as an application of an investigational or nonvalidated therapy, and goverrned by the spirit and ethics that govern research, which are embodied in the process of informed consent. Doctors Moss and LaPuma explain that the use of restraints should be consistent with the overall goals of therapy and that imposing restraints in place of proper medical evaluation, nursing care, and compassion is unethical.

222. Post, Stephen G. Women and Elderly Parents: Moral Controversy in an Aging Society. Hypatia: A Journal of Feminist Philosophy; Spring 1990; 5(1): 83-89.

Post calls attention to the moral problems stemming from a massive demographic transition to an aging society in which the increasing number of the elderly place great pressure on women as caregivers. He exposes the broad range of recent positions on what obligations, if any, adult women owe their parents, as well as the growing social significance of this debate.

223. Pratt, Clara; Schmall, Vicki; Wright, Scott. Ethical Concerns of Family Caregivers to Dementia Patients. Gerontologist; October 1987; 27(5): 632-638.

Family caregivers to dementia patients in Oregon and Washington filled out a questionnaire that identified their major ethical concerns. These concerns included: extent and limits of their filial obligations; conflicting responsibilities to their own spouse, children, and personal needs; finances; standards of care; and the appropriate role of the patient in care planning. These concerns have implications for societal allocation of resources and public policy on autonomy for older persons and their family members.

224. Quinn, Mary J.   Elder Abuse and Neglect Raise New Dilemmas. Generations; Winter 1985; 10(2): 22-25.

This article discusses the ethical dilemmas that confront health care and social service practitioners who must identify and deal with situations of abuse and neglect of older persons. Basic clashes between ethical values of freedom and safety, and the challenge of providing help to nonconsenting older clients, are analyzed. Practical advice for mediating th , e nical tensions is offered.

225. Sabatino, Charles P. Client-Rights Regulations and the Autonomy of Home-Care Consumers. Generations; 1990; 14(Supplement): 21-24.

A number of states have enacted legal bills of rights for home care patients. A seldom asked question is the extent to which such bills of rights are effective in enhancing (of at least preventing diminution of) the autonomy of individuals in long term care.   This paper reports on an American Bar Association exploration of this question. The author offers suggestions for approaches to maximize the positive value of regulation in terms of promoting autonomy.

226. Silliman, Rebecca A. Caring for the Frail Older Patient: The Doctor-Patient-Family Caregiver Relationship. Journal of General Internal Medicine; May/June 1989; 4: 237-241.

The author describes the roles that families play in the care of their frail elders and the effects that caregiving has on family caregivers. This provides the context for a discussion of the doctor-patient-family caregiver relationship. The clinical problem of dementia is used to illustrate ways in which physicians can foster the triadic relationship and, thus, improve the health and functioning of both patient and caregiver.

227. Tehan, Claire. Has Success Spoiled Hospice? Hastings Center Report; October 1985; 15(5): 10-13.

This article describes the social, economic, and organizational forces that exert an impact on the present hospice movement, and examines how these forces affect the ability of the hospice industry to remain true to its original and primary ethical objectives.

228. Young, Patricia Ann. Home-Care Characteristics That Shape the Exercise of Autonomy: A View from the Trenches. Generations; 1990; 14(Supplement): 17-20.

Increases in health care services delivered in the home to a rapidly growing elder population make it imperative that we examine the characteristics unique to home care that enable or disable the exercise of autonomy in health care choices. Three major characteristics that distinguish service delivery to patients in their homes from service delivery in hospitals influence the exercise of autonomy by home care patients. These characteristics are (1) the location of service delivery; (2) the caregiver mix, including both family and formal caregivers; and (3) the interaction between the exercise of autonomy and reimbursement, regulation, environment, and technology in the home care setting.

5
Decisionmaking for Critically Ill
and Suicidal Persons

229. Alzheimer's Disease and Related Disorders Association, Inc. Guidelines for the Treatment of Patients With Advanced Dementia. Chicago, December 10, 1988.

These suggested guidelines emphasize respect for the preferences of patient and family. For many severely and irreversibly demented patients, limitation of life-sustaining medical treatment not relating to comfort may be appropriate. For older patients with mild impairment of memory and cognitive functioning, medical care should be the same as for other elderly patients.

230. American Academy of Neurology, Executive Board. Position of the American Academy of Neurology on Certain Aspects of the Care and Management of the Persistent Vegetative State Patient. Neurology; January 1989; 39(1): 125-126.

Part one of this policy statement discusses the basic medical facts of the persistent vegetative state. Part two explains why artificial nutrition and hydration are forms of medical treatment and why the same factors that govern the withdrawal or withholding of other forms of medical treatment should also apply to artificial nutrition and hydration. Part three supports the fundamental right of patients to make their own treatment decisions and attempts to reconcile potential ethical conflicts between patients/families, on one side, and health care providers, on the other. The final part explains that there are no significant medical or moral distinctions between withholding and withdrawing treatment.

231. American Dietetic Association. Position of the American Dietetic Association: Issues in Feeding the Terminally Ill Adult. Journal of the American Dietetic Association; January 1987; 87(1): 78-85.

This report surveys the ethical, as well as legal, issues involved in withholding or withdrawing artificial means of nutrition and hydration from a dying patient. It concludes that there are circumstances in which forgoing artificial sustenance for some patients is justified. The focus is on the role of the professional dietician in collaborating with the health care team in making recommendations in individual cases.

232. American Geriatrics Society. Position Statement: Medical Treatment Decisions Concerning Elderly Persons. New York; May 1987.

This AGS Position Statement attempts to provide caregivers, patients, and public policymakers with guidance for standards and procedures in dealing with medical decisionmaking for older patients. These guidelines reflect (a) a strong commitment to personal autonomy, (2) both an appreciation of the beneficial potential of modern medicine and honesty regarding its side effects and limitations, and an affirmation of the inestimable value of life and a clear recognition of the inevitability of death.

233. American Medical Association Council on Scientific Affairs and Council on Ethical and Judicial Affairs. Persistent Vegetative State and the Decision to Withdraw or Withhold Life Support. Journal of the American Medical Association; January 19, 1990; 263(3): 426-430.

This AMA report provides criteria for the clinical diagnosis of permanent unconsciousness and reviews the available data that support the reliability of these criteria. Although much of the article traces legal trends in this area, ethical aspects of withdrawal of life support from persons with loss of higher brain function are also mentioned. The ultimate role of the physician in assisting the patient's family or guardian in deciding what is in the patient's best interest is emphasized.

234. American Thoracic Society. Withholding and Withdrawing Life-Sustaining Treatment. Annals of Internal Medicine; September 15, 1991; 115(6): 478-485.

This statement was developed by an ATS Bioethics Task Force. The purpose of the statement is to define acceptable standards of medical practice and make recommendations related to withholding and withdrawing life-sustaining therapy. Specific objectives are: (1) to enhance the understanding of physicians and other health care providers of the ethical and legal issues involved in forgoing life support, (2) to promote medically and ethically sound decision making in clinical practice related to forgoing life support, and (3) to assist in the development of institutional and public policies related to these issues.

235. Angell, Marcia. Euthanasia. New England Journal of Medicine; November 17, 1988; 319(20): 1348-1350.

This article provides background on the issue of purposely terminating the life of a patient to prevent further suffering, looking particularly at the way this question is handled in the Netherlands and in the context of a recent ballot initiative in California. The author outlines some of the ethical arguments for and against active euthanasia.

236. Arras, John D. The Severely Demented, Minimally Functional Patient: An Ethical Analysis. Journal of the American Geriatrics Society; October 1988; 36(10): 938-944.

Philosopher Arras analyzes the difficult problem of medical decisionmaking for a decisionally incompetent but conscious patient. Trying to figure out what the patient would have wanted done (the "subjective" approach) or what course of action would be in the patient's best interests (the "objective" approach) is often a frustrating endeavor. The author suggests as a procedural solution that, when a proposed course of action falls into the gray area of uncertainty, involved and well-intentioned family members should have discretion to decide as they see fit. Justifications for this position are set forth.

237. Baird, Robert M.; Rosenbaum, Stuart E. Euthanasia: The Moral Issues. Buffalo, NY: Prometheus Books; 1989.

This is a collection of published journal articles and book chapters by physicians and philosophers on ethical questions raised by consideration of withholding or withdrawing life-prolonging medical interventions from critically ill patients. Some selections also address the propriety of active hastening of death.

238. Balin, Frances E. The Right to Refuse Treatment: Have We Gone Too Far? Probate Law Journal; 1987; 8: 13-32.

This Comment explores the implications of several judicial decisions in terms of the concepts of suicide and active euthanasia, and argues that the courts have opened the door to the very real possibility of significant abuses. The author urges the courts to exercise substantially more oversight into decisions to remove food and water than they have thus far, so that abuses of the "right to die" can be curtailed.

239. Barondess, Jeremiah A.; Kalb, Paul; Weil, William B., Jr.; Cassel, Christine; Ginzberg, Eli. Clinical Decision-Making in Catastrophic Situations: The Relevance of Age. Journal of the American Geriatrics Society; October 1988; 36(10): 919-937.

This is the report of a 1987 conference convened by the American Geriatrics Society to examine the relevance of a patient's age, at both ends of the spectrum, for ethical issues in clinical decisionmaking for the critically ill. Discussion was structured around the areas of autonomy, surrogacy, and public policy. For the clinician, age often acts as a proxy for other factors, such as health status and prognosis. In terms of public policy, the impact of limited resources for which there are intergenerational rivalries is a major concern, as is the direct role of government in medical decisionmaking.

240. Barry, Robert; Maher, James E. Indirectly Intended Life-Shortening Analgesia: Clarifying the Principles. Issues in Law and Medicine; Fall 1990; 6(2): 117-151.

The authors, a Catholic priest and an anesthesiologist, argue that in most cases it is morally improper to administer forms of analgesia to a patient that are likely to have the side-effect of shortening the patient's life. The article relies heavily on interpretations of Catholic doctrine and the current state of available pain control for critically ill patients.

241. Battin, M. Pabst. The Least Worst Death. Hastings Center Report; April 1983; 13(2): 13-16.

Philosopher Battin suggests that medical decision making for the dying patient rarely breaks down into a simple dichotomy between no treatment at all, on one hand, and aggressive and intrusive intervention, on the other. Rather, there usually is a range of options that can affect the manner (e.g., in terms of pain, dignity, expense) of a patient's dying. The physician has an ethical responsibility to explain these options to patients, and to respect patients' informed choices regarding the medical circumstances of their deaths.

242. Bernards, N.; Bender, D.; Leone, B., editors. Euthanasia: Opposing Viewpoints. San Diego: Greenhaven Press, Inc.; 1989.

Opposing points of view are placed back to back to create a running debate about the ethics of euthanasia, what policy should guide its practice, what criteria should influence euthanasia decisions, and who should make such choices. Contributors to this volme come from backgrounds in medicine, religion, law, philosophy, economics, and political science.

243. Besdine, Richard W. Decisions to Withhold Treatment from Nursing Home Residents. Journal of the American Geriatrics Society; 1983; 31: 602-606.

This article is a relatively early and seminal reflection on the ethical considerations involved in limiting medical intervention for nursing home residents in certain situations. In particular circumstances, respect for the autonomy and beneficence of the resident may argue for withholding or withdrawing life-sustaining medical treatments.

244. Blackhall, Leslie J.; Cobb, Janet; Moskowitz, Mark A. Discussions Regarding Aggressive Care With Critically Ill Patients. Journal of General Internal Medicine; September/October 1989; 4: 399-402.

This study looked at how frequently preferences regarding aggressive care are discussed when patients are admitted to critical care units, who is involved in the discussions, and what patient characteristics are associated with the decision to discuss such issues. Although such discussions occurred more frequently with patients who were elderly, demented, and had poor prognoses and high acuity levels, even those patients' preferences were often not elicited. The authors speculate on why patient preferences were discussed relatively infrequently. They conclude that physicians should engage much more often in frank discussions about treatment options with their patients.

245. Blake, David C. State Interests in Terminating Medical Treatment. Hastings Center Report; May/June 1989; 19(3): 5-13.

Philosopher Blake contends that judicial decisions involving termination of life-sustaining medical treatment have tended to undervalue valid state interests in the preservation of life and maintaining the ethical integrity of the health professions. He urges courts to balance these legitimate interests against individual liberty, rather than assuming that patient autonomy should always prevail. He emphasizes that preservation of life is not absolute, either, but is a factor that must be taken into account in a good ethical weighing process.

246. Bopp, James Jr. Reconciling Autonomy and the Value of Life. Journal of the American Geriatrics Society; May 1990; 38(5): 600-602.

A right-to-life advocate argues that, while the right of a mentally competent patient to refuse medical treatment should be respected, decisions to abate treatment for incompetent patients cannot rightly be made by proxy decisionmakers. Unless the incompetent patient has left clear and convincing instructions while still capable of doing so, Bopp believes that an affirmation of the inestimable value of life compels continued treatment of incompetent patients, including artificial nutrition and hydration.

247. Bradley, Gerard V. Does Autonomy Require Informed and Specific Refusal of Life-Sustaining Medical Treatment? Issues in Law and Medicine; Winter 1989; 5(3): 301-319.

Bradley argues that the principle of autonomy has been overemphasized by courts which have dealt with the issue of termination of life-sustaining medical treatment, especially in cases involving currently incompetent patients. He suggests that society's benevolent interests in protecting the patient have been given too short shrift. He suggests that right-to-die questions should be addressed through societal consensus, decided at the statehouse through the political process, rather than by the courts as a matter of individual autonomy.

248. Brodeur, Dennis. Is a Decision to Forgo Tube Feeding for Another a Decision to Kill? Issues in Law & Medicine; Spring 1991; 6(4): 395-406.

Rev. Brodeur examines the assumptions made in the moral arguments about withholding or withdrawing tube feeding. He contends that there are many cases where it is morally appropriate to discontinue feeding.

249. Brody, Baruch A. Life and Death Decision Making. New York: Oxford University; 1988.

Philosopher Brody attempts to develop and display here a new theory of medical ethics to be applied in arguing about treatment decisions made in the context of critical illness. The five types of moral appeals that constitute his ethical theory are appeals to: consequences (for patients, their families, and others), to rights, to respect for persons, to virtues, and to cost-effectiveness and justice.

250. Brody, Baruch A. Ethical Questions Raised By the Persistent Vegetative Patient. Hastings Center Report; February/March 1988; 18(1): 33-37.

A philosopher analyzes a case example involving a patient in a persistent vegetative state who is being kept alive by various medical interventions and whose family refuses to consider discontinuing these interventions despite the health care team's view that further treatment is futile. Brody raises ethical questions concerning the definition of death and its implications for further interventions, the appropriateness of withdrawing interventions (such as food and fluids and antibiotics) if the family agrees, and the appropriateness of removing interventions or forcing movement of the patient even if the family would object to such actions.

251. Bryce, Sara R.S. Appropriate Care of the Incompetent Older Person: An Ethical Challenge. Issues in Law & Medicine; Summer 1988; 4(1): 69-86.

In this essay, a medical student describes her personal quest for answers to ethical dilemmas in health care for older persons, particularly regarding decisions about life-sustaining medical interventions near the end of life. She argues for a spirit of "maternalism" substituting for the prevailing "paternalism," and for compassion and acceptance of suffering as more professionally virtuous than a premature acquiescence in the end of life. She comments negatively on the ethical training of physicians.

252. Buchanan, Allen E.; Brock, Dan W. Deciding for Others: The Ethics of Surrogate Decision Making. New York: Cambridge University Press; 1990.

Philosophers Buchanan and Broch address issues of decision making for those not capable of choosing for themselves, and offer an ethical framework for developing and evaluating standards in this area. They argue that the family usually should decide for the incompetent patient, as the context in which medical treatment decisions are made--an open institutional environment with caregivers attuned to professional norms and concerned about legal liability--provides significant protection against the possibility of self-interested decision making by families. This book also grapples with the ethical implications of how to evaluate persons for capacity to make medical decisions.

253. Cain, J.; Stacy, L.; Jusenius, K.; Figge, D. The Quality of Dying: Financial, Psychological, and Ethical Dilemmas. Obstetrics & Gynecology; July 1990; 76(1): 149-152.

This article advises gynecologists about communicating with and supporting patients who are terminally ill. The authors address the ethical role of the physician and other members of the health care team in telling the patient bad news, serving the social and psychological needs of patients and families facing transition, and advocating for the patient within the health care system.

254. Callahan, Daniel. Can We Return Death to Disease? Hastings Center Report; January/February 1989; 19(1): Supp 4-6.

Philosopher Callahan opposes active euthanasia and assisted suicide. If the thrust toward these phenomena is to be turned back, he suggests, it will be essential for physicians to address the fear of dying in the company of overly aggressive medical intervention that frightens many people today. It will also be necessary to counteract both the extreme position of patient self-determination that would permit virtually unlimited autonomy and the claim that there is no meaningful ethical distinction between killing another, on one hand, and allowing him or her to die, on the other.

255. Callahan, Daniel. Feeding the Dying Elderly. Generations; Winter 1985; 10(2): 15-17.

In the context of medical decision making about life-sustaining interventions for older patients, Callahan draws an ethical distinction between nutrition and hydration, on one hand, and various forms of medical treatment, on the other. He contends that it may be morally appropriate to withhold or withdraw purely medical treatments when the burdens are likely to be disproportionate to the benefits, but that continuing nutritional support remains morally obligatory.

256. Callahan, Daniel. On Feeding the Dying. Hastings Center Report; October 1983; 13(5): 22.

Callahan agrees with the logic of those who argue that withholding or withdrawing artificial means of nutrition and hydration from decisionally incapacitated patients may be morally permissible in some circumstances. Nonetheless, he pleads strongly for the initiation and continuation of artificial feeding for all patients on an emotional and symbolic basis.

257. Capron, Alexander M. Ironies and Tensions in Feeding the Dying. Hastings Center Report; October 1984; 14(5): 32-35.

Capron examines the ethical issues raised by artificial means of nutrition and hydration for dying patients who cannot speak for themselves. He says that we must acknowledge the symbolic nature of feeding and its importance to our shared mores. Society must protect debilitated people from neglect or abandonment. However, we should not be insensitive to the real or symbolic harm when patients without prospect of recovery or human interaction merely have their deaths prolonged by feeding tubes.

258. Capron, Alexander M. Legal and Ethical Problems in Decisions for Death. La, Medicine & Health Care; September 1986; 14(3-4): 141-144, 157.

Capron discusses four aspects of the abatement of life-sustaining medical treatment question that have ethical consequences: changes in the locale of death, the development of ever more sophisticated technology to sustain life almost indefinitely, free-floating fear of legal liability among providers, and a political polarization of life-support decisions as those issues get swept up in the ferocious battles between freedom-of-choice and right-to-life supporters.

259. Capron, Alexander M. The Burden of Decision. Hastings Center Report; May/June 1990; 20(3): 36-41.

Although there are good reasons for courts to become involved in some bioethics cases, the author finds troubling the increasing proclivity to turn to the courts routinely, especially in treatment termination cases. Capron discusses the several problems that arise when medical decisionmaking is brought into the courtroom instead of being negotiated privately. Courts do their job best when they try to ensure a fair and appropriate process rather than a particular outcome. Typically, this means that a court should be concerned with finding and empowering a competent decisionmaker, whether that be the patient or an appropriate surrogate.

260. Carlon, Graziano C. Quest for the Philosopher's Stone. Critical Care Medicine; May 1989; 17(5): 477-478.

The physician author decries modern unquestioning faith in technological quick fixes and the felt need of physicians to justify the withholding of technological interventions for some patients despite their futility. The burden of proof ought to be reversed.

261. Carmi, A., Editor. Euthanasia. New York: Springer-Verlag; 1984.

This collection of essays presents an array of religious and cultural viewpoints on the subject of active and passive euthanasia, quality of life issues, and the individual's right to die.

262. Cohen, Cynthia B., Editor. Casebook on the Termination of Life-Sustaining Treatment and the Care of the Dying. Bloomington, IN: Indiana University Press; 1988.

This teaching text contains twenty-six case studies that illuminate the range of ethical issues that confront patients, families, health care professionals, and administrators in the process of making medical decisions concerning the initiation, continuation, withholding, or withdrawal of life-sustaining interventions. Specific subjects raised by the case discussions include--among others--resuscitation, Institutional Ethics Committees (IECs), advance directives, and artificial nutrition.

263. Corless, Inge B. Physicians and Nurses: Roles and Responsibilities in Caring for the Critically Ill Patient. Law, Medicine & Health Care; April 1982; 10(2): 72-76.

The author discusses the health care team concept as applied to care of the critically ill patient. The article argues that a reconsideration of the respective roles and relationships of team members will provide a higher quality of service to patients. A reformulation is also justified by the author as important to improving the interaction between physicians, nurses, and other professional groups.

264. Danis, Marion; Patrick, Donald L.; Southerland, Leslie I.; Green, Michael L. Patients' and Families' Preferences for Medical Intensive Care. Journal of the American Medical Association; August 12, 1988; 260(6): 797-802.

This study examined patient and family preferences for intensive care treatment and the importance of quality of life in those treatment preferences. The results indicate that older patients with previous ICU hospitalizations generally are extremely willing to undergo intensive care regardless of their age, functional status, perceived quality of life, hypothetical life expectancy, or the nature of their previous ICU experience. Thus, we cannot assume that quality of life predicts patient preferences for life-sustaining treatment. These findings pose a dilemma in the form of a conflict between individual patient autonomy to choose medical treatment and the principle of maximum welfare, which would justify rationing care to achieve the most total benefit.

265. Degner, Lesley G.; Beaton, Janet I. Life-Death Decisions in Health Care. Washington, DC: Hemisphere Publishing Corporation; 1987.

This book describes how health care professionals and families make medical decisions in situations of critical illness, and how those decisions are influenced by ethical considerations. The authors offer a set of practical criteria to assist in making these difficult decisions near the end of life.

266. Devettere, Raymond J. Reconceptualizing the Euthanasia Debate. Law, Medicine & Health Care; Summer 1989; 17(2): 145-155.

Philosopher Devettere first considers why we tend to interpret withdrawals of life support in terms of conceptually unclear and morally dubious distinctions between causing death and letting die. Instead, he proposes four descriptive categories to distinguish the medical options when the death of a patient is the issue. Finally, the article indicates why a deliberative rather than a deductive kind of moral reasoning is better suited for these descriptive categories.

267. DeWachter, M.A. Active Euthanasia in the Netherlands. Journal of the American Medical Association; 1989; 262: 3316-3319.

This comparative report indicates that the thinking and practice concerning physician assisted suicide is far more developed and open in other western countries, in terms of public and professional tolerance for the concept. At the same time, though, no comprehensive ethical or legal framework has been constructed, and many people remain uncomfortable with the new tolerance.

268. Doerflinger, Richard. Assisted Suicide: Pro-Choice or Anti-Life? Hastings Center Report; January/February 1989; 19(1): Supp 16-19.

The author asserts that autonomy-based arguments in favor of assisted suicide entail a negative statement about the value of life, and that proponents of social and legal acceptance of assisted suicide have not adequately responded to the slippery slope arguments of their opponents. He is especially worried about the psychological vulnerability of elderly and dying patients in the face of an "option" for self-deliverance that many will feel is an obligation.

269. Dresser, Rebecca S.; Robertson, John A. Quality of Life and Non-Treatment Decisions for Incompetent Patients: A Critique of the Orthodox Approach. Law, Medicine & Health Care; Fall 1989; 17(3): 234-244.

This article calls for medical decisions to be made on behalf of decisionally incapacitated persons according to a third party's (ordinarily the family or physician) judgment of what course of action would be in the current interests of the patient. This approach expressly rejects the developing legal trend toward substituted judgment (trying to surmise what the patient would choose if presently capable), even when (perhaps especially when) supplemented by an advance directive. Dresser and Robertson argue that a current interests standard would best protect the patient from both overtreatment and undertreatment.

270. Dyck, Arthur J. Ethical Aspects of Care for the Dying Incompetent. Journal of the American Geriatrics Society; September 1984; 32(9): 661-664.

Philosopher Dyck argues that patients with Alzheimer's disease should have their lives sustained, and that means exist technologically to accomplish this without depriving the patient of basic comfort measures.

271. Emanuel, Ezekiel. A Review of the Ethical and Legal Aspects of Terminating Medical Care. American Journal of Medicine; February 1988; 84(2): 291-301.

This review attempts to clarify some of the ethical and legal (as of late 1987) standards for withholding and withdrawing medical treatment from critically ill patients. Discussion centers on the following questions: (a) Is there a right to refuse medical care? (b) What types of medical care can be terminated? (c) From what types of patients can care be terminated? (d) Who should act as the decision maker? and (e) What are the appropriate criteria for deciding to terminate care?

272. Emanuel, Ezekiel K. A Communal Vision of Care for Incompetent Patients. Hastings Center Report; October/November 1987; 17(5): 15-20.

In making medical treatment decisions for critically ill patients who are not currently capable of making and expressing their own choices and have not left clear advance instructions, families and clinicians generally fall back on the "best interests" standard. This article criticizes this traditional approach as applied on the private, idiosyncratic level, and urges in its place a best interests standard that is formulated on a broader, community-based plane.

273. Engelhardt, H. Tristram Jr. Fashioning an Ethic for Life and Death in a Post-Modern Society. Hastings Center Report; January/February 1989; 19(1): 7-9 Supplement.

For public policy in a secular pluralist society such as the United States, the author asserts, the question is not so much whether voluntary (active) euthanasia is right or wrong, but whether the state may use force to stop competent individuals from being voluntarily euthanized when they do not have special preempting duties to third parties. Engelhardt answers this inquiry that, though one may deplore euthanasia personally, it is not an act for which one can plausibly justify coercive state restraint in general secular terms. In our secular, pluralist society, one will need to accept euthanasia by default.

274. Fentiman, Linda C. Privacy and Personhood Revisited: A New Framework for Substitute Decisionmaking for the Incompetent, Incurably Ill Adult. George Washington Law Review; March 1989; 57(4): 801-848.

This essay focuses on the question of how, and by whom, medical decisions should be made for incompetent, incurably ill adult patients. After an analysis of the sources of the autonomy model for medical decision making and the negative consequences of an exclusive reliance on that model, the author proposes a new framework for making treatment choices for incompetent, incurably ill adults. This model provides maximum opportunities for each individual to determine, without state interference, whether and under what circumstances to accept life-sustaining interventions. Simultaneously, the model recognizes that because all individuals are part of a community, decisionmaking must promote and respect the connectedness of the human family by providing incentives and chances for conversation and compassion.

275. Fletcher, Joseph. The Courts and Euthanasia. Law, Medicine & Health Care; Winter 1987/88; 15(4): 223-230.

Philosopher Fletcher critically analyzes legal treatment (i.e., criminalization) of the practice of active, voluntary euthanasia. He argues that opposition to rational elective dying is logically and ethically untenable. If we accept the end of a dignified death, we should also accept the means to achieve that end. Fletcher chides the law for its faulty moral reasoning on this point, and would decriminalize active euthanasia.

276. Fulop, Milford; Adel, Harold N.; Webster, Ann; Levin, Gilbert. Comparisons of the Reactions of Older and Younger Patients to Intensive Care. Critical Care Medicine; November 1989; 17(11): 1223-1227.

The authors undertook this study to learn whether older patients were more likely than younger to express dismay at having been subjected to uncomfortable invasive procedures in the intensive care or coronary care units, even if those procedures were necessary to save their lives. The authors anticipated that many patients would object, but for most the outcome was just the opposite, regardless of age. The overwhelming majority of patients said they would accept similar treatments in the future, if needed. On average, there was no significant difference in attitude toward future treatment between younger and older patients. There was no relation between the severity or intensity of interventions and the patients' satisfaction or feelings about their treatment, regardless of age. As a matter of ethics and health policy, we should not equate advanced age with serious disability and unhappiness or unwillingness to continued living.

277. Gardner, Karen, Editor. Quality of Life for the Terminally Ill: An Examination of the Issues. Chicago: Joint Commission on Accreditation of Hospitals; 1985.

This is a multidisciplinary collection of articles from Quality Review Bulletin that cover many aspects of hospice care, including ethical and legal questions in decision making, pain control, continuity of care, and financing of services.

278. Gibson, Count D., Jr. Perimortal Initiatives: Issues in Foregoing Life-Sustaining Treatment, Suicide, and Assisted Suicide. Issues in Law and Medicine; 1987; 3(1): 29-35.

The author surveys the spectrum of relationships among the different actors and the subjects of treatment limitation, suicide, and assisted suicide by constructing a matrix to locate relevant ethical and legal issues. He notes as currently controversial issues: the status of food and water as medical care, the status of life as a gift from the divine or a subject of autonomous choice, sanctity versus quality of life, the significance of intentions, the dangers of stereotyping, the secular versus religious character of medical ethics, the physician's role, and the impact of economics on decision making.

279. Gillick, Muriel R. Limiting Medical Care: Physicians' Beliefs, Physicians' Behavior. Journal of the American Geriatrics Society; August 1988; 36(8): 747-752.

This essay describes a physician's perspective on how the majority of clinicians actually limit life-sustaining medical treatment for patients today, what physicians believe about this issue, and why they act as they do. Although physicians rarely articulate the underlying ethical principles in conventional philosophical terms, they nonetheless, in Gillick's view, have a fairly cogent idea of what constitutes ethically appropriate medical care. The author illustrates points with the use of hypothetical examples involving older patients in both acute care and nursing home settings. Comment is made on the frequent discrepancy between doctors' belief in limiting treatment based on prognosis and functional status, on one hand, and overly agressive medical action based on fear of social sanction, on the other.

280. Goetzler, Renee M.; Moskowitz, Mark A. Changes in Physician Attitudes Toward Limiting Care of Critically Ill Patients. Archives of Internal Medicine; August 1991; 151: 1537-1540.

Physicians (teachers and residents) were surveyed in 1981 and 1988, and the results of the two surveys are compared here. In 1988, more respondents expressed comfort in discussing "Do Not Resuscitate" (DNR) status with patients and were more likely to follow a critically ill patient's choice to refuse treatment. In both years, respondents denied that financial factors should be taken into account. Residents were inclined to be less aggressive in treatment in 1988 than earlier. Overall, physician attitudes toward treatment of the critically ill had undergone marked change during the 1980s.

281. Goodwin, James S. Mercy Killing: Mercy for Whom? Journal of the American Medical Association; January 16, 1991; 265(3): 326.

The physician author argues against active euthanasia of persons with Alzheimer's disease. Such action, he suggests, is not altruistic for the patient, but rather responds to the suffering and misery of the patient's family.

282. Gordon, Geoffrey H.; Tolle, Susan W. Discussing Life-Sustaining Treatment: A Teaching Program for Residents. Archives of Internal Medicine; March 1991; 151: 567-570.

This article describes an educational initiative at Oregon Health Sciences University designed to help medical residents learn how to communicate better with patients about preferences for life-sustaining medical interventions before the onset of cognitive impairment or a life-threatening illness. Discussions about advance directives was simulated with volunteers. This educational program represents a successful model that could be replicated elsewhere.

283. Gorovitz, Samuel. Drawing the Line: Life, Death, and Ethical Choices in an American Hospital. New York: Oxford University Press; 1991.

Based on his seven weeks experience as an observer at a major teaching hospital, philosopher Gorovitz ruminates on many of the ethical issues confronting providers of acute medical services. Several chapters deal specifically with the elderly, including "Very Ill and Very Old" and "At the End of Life." Particular issues explored include the propriety of cardiopulmonary resuscitation, withholding and withdrawing other life-sustaining interventions, and allocation of scarce resources.

284. Green, Willard. Setting Boundaries for Artificial Feeding. Hastings Center Report; December 1984; 14(6): 8-10.

This article reports on a 1984 conference of the Society for Health and Human Values designed to begin to set some ethical boundaries around decisions to forgo artificial feeding and hydration for critically ill patients. Discussion aimed at setting boundaries around the right of a patient to refuse feeding for himself or herself, the right of surrogates to decide for a patient, and around the economic and social pressures that might influence decisions in this realm.

285. Grisez, Germain. Should Nutrition and Hydration Be Provided to Permanently Unconscious and Other Mentally Disabled Persons? Issues in Law and Medicine; Fall 1989; 5(2): 165-179.

This article addresses the issue of whether artificial nutrition and hydration should be provided to persons who are permanently unconscious or otherwise severely mentally disabled. The author answers in the affirmative, claiming that nutrition and hydration should continue to be provided because it keeps these persons alive and maintains human solidarity with them.

286. Gunn, Albert E. Risk-Benefit Ratio: The Soft Underbelly of Patient Autonomy. Issues in Law and Medicine; Fall 1991; 7(2): 139-153.

The author contends that vulnerable, decisionally incapacitated patients are jeopardized in medical treatment decisionmaking by the use of risk-benefit (burden/benefit) ratios under the guise of promoting patient autonomy. Attorney/physician Gunn believes that the risk-benefit principle is just a rhetorical device to shift authority back to the physician, who may misuse it by withholding or withdrawing life-sustaining medical treatment without moral justification.

287. Hamner, James E. III; Jacobs, Barbara J., Editors. Life and Death Issues. Memphis: University of Tennessee Press; 1986.

This set of Proceedings from a 1985 conference contains essays on health care rationing, medical treatment at the end of life, and health care cost containment. Prominent philosophers and physicians are contributors.

288. Hanson, Laura C.; Danis, Marion. Use of Life-Sustaining Care for the Elderly. Journal of the American Geriatrics Society; August 1991; 39(8): 772-777.

Advanced age has been proposed as one criterion for limiting the use of life-sustaining medical treatment. The authors retrospectively studied utilization rates of intensive care, and found that it is utilized less frequently prior to death (i.e., for terminal hospitalizations) for patients over seventy-five, based on diagnosis and functional status as well as chronological age. Potential explanations for the disparity in intensive care use based on age include physicians using chronological age itself as an exclusion criterion, irreversible disease states or poor functional status being more common among elderly inpatients, and older patients themselves preferring limits to be placed on aggressive medical care.

289. Harris, Curtis E.; Bostrom, Barry A. Is the Continued Provision of Food and Fluids in Nancy Cruzan's Best Interests? Issues in Law & Medicine; Spring 1990; 5(4): 415-435.

These authors argue that, even for persons living in a permanently unconscious or noncommunicative state, tube feeding constitutes a more fundamental form of human care than medical intervention. Continued tube feeding, they assert, is always morally obligatory because it is in the best interests of such persons.

290. Hastings Center. Guidelines on the Termination of Life-Sustaining Treatment and the Care of the Dying. Briarcliff Manor, NY: Hastings Center; 1987.

This report of a project by a prominent bioethics thinktank represents a consensus statement of principles concerning decision making regarding life-sustaining medical interventions. The Guidelines are predicated on a solid presumption in favor of medical treatment and life, with a decision to limit intervention constituting an exception requiring compelling justification in the context of a particular case. One finds here a robust commitment to a patient-centered ethic , founded on the individual's right to make autonomous medical choices. There is also a rejection of financial factors, by themselves, as the predicate for limiting access to treatment for a patient who might benefit from the treatment and who desires it.

291. Hoyt, Jane D.; Davies, James M. A Response to the Task Force on Supportive Care. Law, Medicine & Health Care; June 1984; 12(3): 103-105, 134.

These representatives of an advocacy organization for nursing home residents object to recommendations for institutional policies that would permit the provision of supportive medical care only for certain persons. They argue that such policies would unfairly jeopardize the rights and welfare--indeed, the lives--of decisionally incapacitated and disabled nursing home residents. Instead, they urge aggressive, life-prolonging medical interventions for residents as ethically and socially compelled.

292. Ikuta, Sandra S. Dying at the Right Time: A Critical Legal Theory Approach to Timing-of-Death Issues. Issues in Law and Medicine; Summer 1989; 5(1): 3-66.

This article argues that the law lacks capacity to deal effectively, i.e., to guide behavior, with issues concerning withholding or withdrawal of life-prolonging medical treatment. Legal discourse cannot guarantee that decisions will be made lovingly by a caring decisionmaker, which is the patient's only protection from abuse. The author suggests that the solution to right-to-die questions must come not from legislation or adjudication, but from the emergence of a stronger societal consensus about what constitutes a good death.

293. Jecker, Nancy S. Giving Death a Hand: When the Dying and the Doctor Stand in a Special Relationship. Journal of the American Geriatrics Society; August 1991; 39(8): 831-835.

This paper considers the possibility that, under special circumstances, physicians who stand in a close personal relationship with a patient are ethically permitted to actively assist their patient in dying. Viewed from the perspective of the costs born by patients, families, and health providers when terminally ill patients are left to languish and suffer, Jecker contends that the love and care one harbors for a particular dying person may impel one to intervene and hasten death.

294. Johnson, Dana E. Withholding Fluids and Nutrition: Identifying the Populations at Risk. Issues in Law & Medicine; 1986; 2(3): 189-201.

This article discusses the labels that are affixed to patients by the medical staff and how those labels create populations that are at risk for being deprived of life-sustaining food and fluids. The discussion highlights the problems associated with the use of such labels and identifies the need to rigorously define and understand these terms which appear to play such a large part in persuading decisionmakers to limit treatment.

295. Jonsen, Albert R. Beyond the Physicians' Reference: The Ethics of Active Euthanasia. Western Journal of Medicine; August 1988; 149(2): 195-198.

Philosopher Jonsen questions the validity of traditional philosophical arguments, based on ethical principles and theories, opposing the physician's personal involvement in actively hastening the death of a patient. However, Jonsen asserts that participation in active euthanasia would offend the physician's proper role because the hastening of a patient's death is not a matter requiring the particular skill and knowledge of a physician.

296. Jonsen, Albert R. What Does Life Support Support? Pharos; Winter 1987; 50(1): 4-7.

This article looks at the ethical and philosophical issues that arise in the context of providing artificial life support to patients, especially as the nature of that support has evolved from partial to total and from temporary to permanent.

297. Kapp, Marshall B. Termination of Treatment: A Legal Update. Alabama Journal of Medical Sciences; 1988; 25(1): 91-95.

This article reviews legal cases based on termination of life-sustaining medical intervention issues. Ethical principles underlying and informing legal trends in the "right to die" area are identified. Suggestions for keeping termination of treatment decisions a personal, rather than a legal, matter are offered.

298. Kapp, Marshall B. Family Decision-Making for Nursing Home Residents: Legal Mechanisms and Ethical Underpinnings. Theoretical Medicine; 1987; 8: 259-273.

This article looks at the question of surrogate or proxy medical decisionmaking by families on behalf of mentally incapable nursing home residents. Discussed are methods of delegation of authority from a resident to a family member: by advance planning; by operation of statute, regulation, or judicial precedent; by custom or convention; or by court order.   The ethical principles underlying both the selection of a proxy decisionmaker and the making of specific treatment choices is explicated.

299. Kapp, Marshall B. Ethics vs. Fear of Malpractice. Generations; Winter 1985; 10(2): 18-20.

The author demonstrates how fixation on legal liability considerations by physicians and other human service providers in the context of medical treatment decisionmaking for older patients can lead to actions that, ironically, are harmful ethically to the patient. By attempting to dispel some of this anxiety and suggest constructive risk management strategies, this article aims to encourage provider behavior that more ethically serves the interests of seriously ill older persons.

300. Kass, Leon R. Death With Dignity and the Sanctity of Life. Commentary; March 1990; 90: 33-43.

In discussing questions about medical treatment near the end of life, Kass rejects the language of rights and duties. He also rejects the idea that the concepts of death with dignity and sanctity of life are opposed and require a choice between them. For him, the two concepts are complementary. He argues that both concepts are compatible with letting die but not with deliberate killing. He also urges against active euthanasia, on both secular and religious grounds.

301. Kass, Leon R. Neither Love Nor Money: Why Doctors Must Not Kill. The Public Interest; Winter 1989; (94): 25-46.

Kass argues forcefully against physician participation in active euthanasia and assisted suicide. Such participation, he contends, violates our basic expectations and aspirations about medicine and the role of physicians.

302. Kayser-Jones, Jeanie. The Use of Nasogastric Feeding Tubes in Nursing Homes: Patient, Family and Health Care Provider Perspectives. Gerontologist; August 1990; 30(4): 469-479.

A nurse-anthropologist studied the attitudes of patients, family members, nurses, and physicians regarding the use of tube feeding in three nursing homes. The author recommends better communication among the various parties regarding decisions about feeding tubes. She also concludes that more thorough patient evaluation would assist greatly in the decisionmaking process.

303. Kinsella, T. Douglas; Stocking, Carol B. Failed Communication About Life-Support Therapy: Silent Physicians and Mute Patients. American Journal of Medicine; June 1989; 86: 643-644.

This editorial makes three points about decision making about life-sustaining medical interventions. First, the communication gap about aggressive life-support therapy is created both by physicians and by patients. Second, since the preferences of patients about life-sustaining therapy seem more changeable than is generally believed, the periodic reaffirmation of such preferences must be sought aggressively by physicians. Third, there is an urgent need for further research to define those characteristics of both patients and physicians that generate their behaviors in these situations.

304. Kohn, Martin; Menon, Geeta. Life Prolongation: Views of Elderly Outpatients and Health Care Professionals. Journal of the American Geriatrics Society; September 1988; 36(9): 840-844.

This study used a qualitative research design to explore factors that influence older patients and health care professionals in making life-prolongation decisions. Common criteria cited by both groups were clinical considerations, patients' wishes, age, and a pragmatic approach to the consequences. Communication between physicians and their older patients regarding life-prolongation decisions was found wanting, with both parties reluctant to bring up the matter with each other but quite ready to discuss these issues with others.

305. Koop, C. Everett. The Challenge of Definition. Hastings Center Report; January/February 1989; 19(1): Supp 2-3.

The Surgeon General argues that potential "Granny Does" should be given all indicated medical treatment, which means at least providing her with the nutrition and fluids needed to sustain life at its most basic level. If the patient were in the final stages of a terminal illness, Dr. Koop would prescribe basic nutrition and fluids and "then stand back to let nature take its course." He rebels against what he describes as "the terror of the euthanasian ethic."

306. Kuhse, Helga. The Case for Active Voluntary Euthanasia. Law, Medicine & Health Care; September 1986; 14(3-4): 145-148.

An Australian philosopher argues that there is no ethically valid distinction between active, voluntary euthanasia and passive euthanasia (withholding or withdrawing life-sustaining medical care from a critically ill patient). Therefore, she contends, principles of patient autonomy and well-being lead to a conclusion condoning the active, intentional hastening of a patient's death where the patient has requested such assistance.

307. Kuhse, Helga; Singer, Peter. Doctors' Practices and Attitudes Regarding

Voluntary Euthanasia. Medical Journal of Australia; June 20, 1988; 148: 623-627.

The authors surveyed Australian physicians and discovered a clear majority who supported active voluntary euthanasia, many who had provided active help in bringing about a patient's death, and many more who would engage in such practices if they were legal. Among the different reasons physicians were asked to hasten death, "infirmities of old age" ranked high on the list. The level of support for active euthanasia among Australian physicians in this survey was higher than the level recorded among their British counterparts in an earlier survey. The authors present some of the ethical arguments for and against amending the law to explicitly condone active voluntary euthanasia.

308. Landsman, Ron M. Helping the Hopelessly Ill. Trusts and Estates; April 1988; 127(4): 37-42.

The attorney-author outlines the essentially moral issues and strategies for attorneys to review and consider in attempting to secure an agreement between families and medical providers to terminate medical treatment that is no longer appropriate for the patient. The article also speaks to institutional--hospital and nursing home--counsel seeking to honor patient and family moral wishes without undue exposure to regulatory, criminal, or civil liability.

309. LaPuma, John; Schiedermayer, David L.; Toulmin, Stephen; Miles, Steven H.; McAtee, Jane A. The Standard of Care: A Case Report and Ethical Analysis. Annals of Internal Medicine; January 1988; 108(1): 121-124.

Using the case of an older, critically ill patient as a reference point, the authors illustrate how apprehension about possible legal liability sometimes can impel the health care team toward conduct that violates sound clinical judgment and good ethics. They explore the value of ethics consultations in helping to overcome legal anxiety and make appropriate moral decisions about treatment near the end of the patient's life.

310. Larue, Gerald A. Euthanasia and Religion: A Survey of the Attitudes of World Religions to the Right-to-Die. Los Angeles: Hemlock Society; 1985.

This pamphlet records the results of a questionnaire distributed by the

Hemlock Society, which advocates the ethical and legal right to assisted suicide and active and passive euthanasia. The book serves as a guide to announced positions of a wide number of religions on questions of passive and active euthanasia.

311. Lee, Melinda A. Depression and Refusal of Life Support in Older People: An Ethical Dilemma. Journal of the American Geriatrics Society; June 1990; 38(6): 710-714.

This article discusses ethical dilemmas that arise when a physician must decide whether to respect the refusal of life-sustaining medical treatment by a clinically depressed older patient. Using analysis of a case example, the author shows how the usual medical practice of identifying and treating conditions that transiently impair decisionmaking capacity before deciding to withhold or withdraw life-sustaining medical intervention entails another ethical problem: denying the depressed patient the right to refuse unwanted interventions in the meantime.

312. Levkoff, Sue; Wetle, Terrie. Clinical Decision Making in the Care of the Aged. Journal of Aging and Health; February 1989; 1(1): 83-101.

This study involved telephone interviews with Veterans Administration physicians, nurses, and social workers testing reactions to two factual vignettes. The goals of the study were (1) to identify the determinants of specific clinical decisions involving geriatric patients (including ethical, medical, legal, social, and institutional factors), (2) to describe how health care providers use and weigh information in their clinical decision making, and (3) to assess whether the determinants of those decisions are consistent among physicians, nurses, and social workers, and across different types of decisions. The investigators found that age, when separated from expected quality of life, was not a consistent predictor of outcomes across professions in either vignette.

313. Lipsky, Martin S.; Hickey, Daniel P.; Bworning, Gale; Taylor, Christine. The Use of Do-Not-Hospitalize Orders by Family Physicians in Ohio. Journal of Family Practice; 1990; 30(1): 61-64.

The authors surveyed Ohio family practitioners by mail to determine prevailing knowledge, attitudes, and practices regarding the use of Do Not Hospitalize (DNH) orders in nursing homes. This article reports on the most common reasons for using or not using such orders. The authors cautiously suggest that familiarizing more physicians with the DNH concept may yield positive results both in terms of enhancing resident autonomy and conserving general health care resources.

314. Lo, Bernard; Dornbrand, Laurie. Understanding the Benefits and Burdens of Tube Feedings. Archives of Internal Medicine; September 1989; 149(9): 1925-1926.

Artificial feedings might benefit patients by reversing malnutrition or dehydration and prolonging life in patients who are unable to take adequate nutrition by mouth. But feeding tubes may not accomplish these goals and may impose significant burdens on patients with severe, irreversible illness. Physicians Lo and Dornbrand urge that tube feedings should be given only when the benefit to the patient is likely to exceed the burden and when informed consent has been obtained. Tube feedings should not be considered "ordinary" (i.e., always morally obligatory) care.

315. Loewy, Erich H. Weakening the Bonds of Friendship: An Unfortunate Outcome of the Cruzan Decisions. Journal of the American Geriatrics Society; January 1991; 39(1): 98-100.

This paper deals with the effects of the Missouri and United States Supreme Courts' decisions in the Cruzan case, concerning surrogate decision making about withholding or withdrawing life-prolonging medical interventions for mentally incompetent persons. Dr. Loewy fears that the Cruzan decisions will further weaken the physician/patient/surrogate relationship. He examines the role of theoretical ethics, justice-based reasoning, and care-based reasoning in dealing with individual medical care decision making situations.

316. Loewy, Erich H. Changing One's Mind: When Is Odysseus to Be Believed? Journal of General Internal Medicine; January/February 1988; 3(1): 54-58.

This article discusses the ethical dilemma of medical decision making, particularly in critical illness situations, where the patient appears to change his or her mind. Dr. Loewy sets forth the general principle that, when decisions conflict and when both can be considered to be approximately equal autonomous choices, the more recent decision should be followed. In more troubling cases, though, we should ask not only which decision is more recent, but which judgment truly represents the patient's autonomous will. If one considers autonomy to be the capacity for independent thought, decision, or action, one will have to be guided by an assessment of the validity of the prior compared to the present choice.

317. Luce, John M. Ethical Principles in Critical Care. Journal of the American Medical Association; February 2, 1990; 263(5): 696-700.

Dr. Luce applies the ethical principles of beneficence, nonmaleficence, autonomy, disclosure, and social justice to several common critical care issues.   These include medical decision making, informed consent, resuscitation, brain death and organ transplantation, withholding and withdrawing life support, and the allocation of medical resources.

318. Luce, John M.; Raffin, Thomas A. Withholding and Withdrawal of Life Support from Critically Ill Patients. Chest; September 1988; 94(3): 621-626.

This article examines withholding and withdrawal of life support from an Intensive Care Unit perspective. It begins with a historic review and then discusses evolving concepts of life and death in American society, legal implications, the use of advance directives, medical attitudes regarding limitation of treatment, and the ways in which treatment limitation occurs.

319. Lynn, Joanne, Editor. By No Extraordinary Means: The Choice to Forgo Life-Sustaining Food and Water. Bloomington, IN: Indiana University Press; 1986.

A 1984 interdisciplinary symposium resulted in this collection of essays dealing with the ethical, as well as the clinical, religious, legal, and public policy, aspects of decisions to cease artificial nutrition and hydration for dying persons.

320. Lynn, Joanne; Childress, James F. Must Patients Always Be Given Food and Water? Hastings Center Report; October 1983; 13(5): 17-21.

The authors argue that there exist situations where it is ethically permissible to discontinue artificial means of nutrition and hydration for an incompetent patient. The same criteria should apply here, they suggest, as for other forms of medical intervention. Removal of artificial feeding is condoned where its continuation would be futile, there is no possibility of benefit, or the burdens would be disproportionate to any likely benefits. Continuation of tube feeding in such circumstances is not required under any obligation to provide "ordinary" care, to continue care that has been started, or to provide symbolic treatment.

321. MacLean, Susan L. The Decision-Making Process in Critical Care of the Aged. Critical Care Nursing Quarterly; 1989; 12(1): 74-81.

The purpose of this article is to enhance the decisionmaking abilities of nurses who care for elderly patients in a critical care setting by providing information about variables that may influence optimal decision making and by describing strategies for more objective and systematic decision making. Clinical variables that influence the judgment process and outcomes include the clinician's knowledge and experiences, information-processing ability, cognitive biases; and attitudes, values, and stereotypic beliefs. Also discussed are task variables and patient variables (including age) that influence nurses in critical care.

322. May, William E.; Barry, Robert; Griese, Orville; et. al. Feeding and Hydrating the Permanently Unconscious and Other Vulnerable Persons. Issues in Law & Medicine; 1987; 3(3): 203-217.

This statement is a working document prepared by its drafters for the Pope John XXIII Center, which studies bioethical issues. It is endorsed by signatories from many religious backgrounds. The statement concludes that foregoing artificially provided foods and fluids for people with even severe disabilities cannot be ethically justified, except perhaps under extraordinary circumstances, because of the intrinsic value of human life and the relatively minor burdens imposed by providing such sustenance.

323. McCartney, James J.; Trau, Jane Mary. Cessation of the Artificial Delivery of Food and Fluids: Defining Terminal Illness and Care. Death Studies; 1990; 14(5): 435-444.

Relying on "common sense" and the Roman Catholic tradition, the authors conclude that: (1) the permanently unconscious are necessarily terminally ill; (2) useless or burdensome medical treatment is rightly withheld or withdrawn from the terminally ill; and (3) care provided to the permanently unconscious sometimes is burdensome, and thus may be rightly refused.

324. Meilaender, Gilbert. On Removing Food and Water: Against the Stream. Hastings Center Report; December 1984; 14(6): 11-13.

A philosopher presents arguments in opposition to the ethical propriety of discontinuing artificial nutrition and hydration for permanently unconscious patients. Meilander submits that feeding is morally distinguishable from other forms of medical intervention, and that the reasons justifying discontinuation of the latter do not apply to the former.

325. Meyers, Roberta M.; Grodin, Michael A. Decisionmaking Regarding the Initiation of Tube Feedings in the Severely Demented Elderly: A Review. Journal of the American Geriatrics Society; May 1991; 39(5): 526-531.

This article compares and contrasts decisionmaking concerning the initiation of tube feedings for the severely demented elderly with the process of deciding about withdrawal of tube feedings from patients in a persistent vegetative state. The authors examine the role and limits of the ethical principles of autonomy and beneficence in this context. They urge deference to the role of the family as surrogate decisionmaker for incapacitated elders, but also outline the place of physicians, nurses, other caregivers, and institutions in the decisional process. The important elements in developing decisionmaking guidelines are discussed, and tolerance for a plurality of outcomes is requested.

326. Michelson, Carole; Mulvihill, Michael; Hsu, Ming-Ann; Olson, Ellen. Eliciting Medical Care Preferences from Nursing Home Residents. Gerontologist; June 1991; 31(3): 358-363.

This survey was designed to elicit medical treatment preferences from healthy, alert nursing home residents, by asking them about hypothetical treatment choices frequently encountered in the nursing home setting. On the whole, study participants were opposed to aggressive medical intervention except where it would alleviate pain or result in greater patient comfort or safety. This reaction was especially pronounced when participants were confronted with questions concerning the treatment of debilitated elderly patients with dementia. Understanding patient preferences and encouraging their advance documentation can help caregivers and families to engage in better ethical decision making and conduct on behalf of patients who have become incapacitated.

327. Miles, Steven H.; Singer, Peter A.; Siegler, Mark. Conflicts Between Patients' Wishes to Forgo Treatment and the Policies of Health Care Facilities. New England Journal of Medicine; July 6, 1989; 321(1): 48-50.

This article explores the ethical dilemma that erupts when a health care institution has enunciated a treatment philosophy that is incompatible with a patient's or family's request to discontinue life support. The authors review three court cases addressing this issue, consider whether the administration of a facility may decline to comply with a request to forgo life-sustaining treatment, and examine the ethical options in such situations.

328. Miller, Bruce L. Autonomy and the Refusal of Lifesaving Treatment. Hastings Center Report; August 1981; 11(4): 22-28.

Philosopher Miller uses four hypothetical cases to illustrate four different senses of the ethical principle of autonomy as applied to the refusal of lifesaving medical treatment: free action, authenticity, effective deliberation, and moral reflection. Discussion focuses on resolving apparent conflicts among these four senses, and on bridging the concepts of autonomy and paternalism in clinical care of patients.

329. Miller, Tracy; Cugliari, Anna M. Withdrawing and Withholding Treatment: Policies in Long-Term Care Facilities. Gerontologist; August 1990; 30(4): 462-468.

This article reports on a set of surveys of nursing homes in New York conducted by that state's Task Force on Life and the Law. Data were collected regarding institutional policies on limitation of medical care, decisionmaking processes, prevalence of institutional ethics committees and other vehicles for mediating disagreements, and policies on advance directives. Not surprisingly, the 1988 survey (conducted after enactment of

New York's statute on CPR in health care facilities) indicated wider development and implementation of written policies and formal dispute mediation structures than was reported in the 1986 survey.

330. Molloy, David W.; Clarnette, Roger M.; Braun, E. Ann; Eisemann, Martin R.; Sneiderman, B. Decision Making in the Incompetent Elderly: The Daughter from California Syndrome. Journal of the America Geriatrics Society; April 1991; 39(4): 396-399.

This case report illustrates some of the ethical quandaries that can appear when decisions regarding life-sustaining medical interventions must be made for an older, decisionally incapable patient who has not left an advance directive to guide the family or the physician.

331. Murphy, Donald J.; Lynn, Joanne. Care Near the End of Life. in: Cassel, Christine K.; Riesenberg, Donald E.; Sorenson, Leif B.; Walsh, John R., Editors. Geriatric Medicine. 2nd ed. New York: Springer-Verlag; 1990: 607-614.

In addition to discussing clinical factors, these two geriatricians explore some of the ethical and social policy issues involved in caring for dying patients. They urge a realistic assessment of the likely efficacy of therapeutic possibilities and respect for the patient's self-determination and best interests. Considerations of distributive justice, allocation of scarce resources, and the effects of decisions on other parties are also mentioned, as is the moral conundrum of euthanasia.

332. Nolan, Kathleen. Do-Not-Hospitalize Orders: Whose Goals? What Purpose? Journal of Family Practice; 1990; 30(1): 31-32.

The author urges caution regarding the use of Do Not Hospitalize (DNH) orders in nursing homes. A DNH order may issue a sweeping injunction against a wide range of possible future medical interventions. Such an order is problematic because making responsible decisions about what interventions to use or forgo generally requires first specifying the relation of the proposed treatment to the patient's overall management goal. DNH orders in nursing homes provide an excellent framework for involving residents and their families in serious discussions about future treatment. Clinicians, in consultation with residents and families, must develop and articulate management plans that are more than a string of shalls and shall nots.

333. Nosal, Roger A. Helping Patients Prepare for Death. Senior Patient; January/February 1989: 116-120.

A family physician uses two case examples to illustrate ethical issues that arise for the doctor in caring for patients near the end of life. He emphasizes the physician's role in empowering the patient to participate in decisionmaking.

334. Office of the Vicar General (Archdiocese of New York); Monsignor Sheridan. Principles in Regard to Withholding or Withdrawing Artificially Assisted Nutrition/Hydration. 1011 First Avenue, New York, NY; November 16, 1989.

This statement of principles from the New York Archdiocese focuses on the ethical implications of limiting artificial feeding for the permanently unconscious but nondying patient. It examines the issue by balancing the reasonableness of burdens associated with treatment against likely benefits to the patient.

335. Orentlicher, David. Physician Participation in Assisted Suicide. Journal of the American Medical Association; 1989; 262: 1844-1845.

Deeply rooted medical traditions and the guiding principles of medical ethics say that a physician should not assist the suicide of a patient, regardless of condition. The possibility of assisted suicide might undermine the patient's trust that the physician is completely devoted to caring for the patient's health. Moreover, the critically ill patient might not be able to resist a physician's suggestion that suicide be considered as an appropriate option.

336. O'Rourke, Kevin. Should Nutrition and Hydration Be Provided to Permanently Unconscious and Other Mentally Disabled Persons? Issues in Law and Medicine; Fall 1989; 5(2): 181-196.

A Catholic priest answers the question posed in the article's title in the negative. He argues that the standards published by various medical organizations and the official teaching of the Church permit the withholding of nutrition and hydration from persons who are permanently comatose. O'Rourke contends that withholding nutrition and hydration is ethically justified because such feeding not only provides no benefit to the person, but constitutes a significant burden.

337. Ouslander, Joseph G.; Tymchuk, Alexander J.; Rahbar, Bita. Health Care Decisions Among Elderly Long-Term Care Residents and Their Potential Proxies. Archives of Internal Medicine; June 1989; 149(6): 1367-1372.

This study found a considerable discordance between medical decisions actually made by long-term care residents and the decisions their potential proxies thought they would make. Most elderly long term care residents have failed to complete a formal advance directive, and their preferences are often unknown to family and health care providers. The authors implore primary care physicians involved with the frail elderly to encourage early and ongoing dialogue between their elderly patients, close relatives, and key interdisciplinary team members in long-term care settings, such as nurses and social workers.

338. Park Ridge Center for the Study of Health, Faith and Ethics. Active Euthanasia, Religion and the Public Debate. Chicago: Park Ridge Center; 1991.

This volume opens with case studies in which aid in dying is sought. The next section reviews arguments for and against suicide and active euthanasia, and explains the issues, their origins, and common terms in this debate. Included are summaries of the attitudes of various faith traditions toward active euthanasia. The final section explores the public policy implications of this ethical discussion.

339. Pearlman, Robert A.; Uhlmann, Richard F. Quality of Life in Elderly, Chronically Ill Outpatients. Journal of Gerontology--Medical Sciences; March 1991; 46(2): M31-38.

Health care providers and researchers frequently use objective indicators, such as age and marital status, to make judgments about a patient's quality of life. In a large scale interview of older, chronically ill outpatients in three different settings, however, these authors found that objective indicators correlated poorly with the older patients' own perceptions of quality of life. Instead, subjective factors are most influential for older patients' perceptions of their emotional, socioeconomic, intellectual, and physical functioning. The lesson is that treating physicians must investigate their patients' subjective ratings of these domains in their lives when treatment alternatives and patient choices regarding medical care are discussed.

340. Pearlman, Robert A.; Uhlmann, Richard F. Perceptions of Quality of Life in Elderly Patients With Cardiovascular Disease. Quality of Life and Cardiovascular Care; May/June 1986: 149-158.

The authors compared how elderly patients with cardiovascular disease and their physicians respectively assessed patient quality of life. Physicians focused on considerations of physical health, discomfort, mood, and functional impairments and consistently rated quality of life lower than patients, who tended to concentrate more on physical health and discomfort. This disparity is important, because quality of life assessments often figure into geriatric treatment decisions, especially concerning such matters as CPR and other life-sustaining interventions.

341. Poses, Roy M.; Bekes, Carolyn; Copare, Fiore J.; Scott, William E. The Answer to 'What Are My Chances, Doctor?' Depends on Whom Is Asked: Prognostic Disagreement and Inaccuracy for Critically Ill Patients. Critical Care Medicine; August 1989; 17(8): 827-833.

One of the most difficult problems in the area of communication and medical decisionmaking concerning critically ill patients is the unreliability of physician prognoses regarding the patient's likely medical fate. This article documents and discusses this problem and its implications.

342. Post, Stephen G. Severely Demented Elderly People: A Case Against Senicide. Journal of the American Geriatrics Society; June 1990; 38(6): 715-718.

Philosopher Post argues against senicide--the deliberate killing of severely demented older persons. These persons have not ceased to live in a biographical sense, an ethical society should maintain a general prohibition against killing, and destroying the severely demented would send a negative message to older persons who are dependent on others. Severely demented older persons should be provided with basic custodial care designed to minimize anxiety and distress and to support the person emotionally, although life-sustaining technologies should be employed rarely for this population.

343. Potts, Stephen. Looking for the Exit Door: Killing and Caring in Modern Medicine. Houston Law Review; May 1988; 25: 493-515.

Dr. Potts concedes that the argument to legalize active euthanasia is powerful, but he concludes that in the end it fails. Individual cases are insufficient, he finds, to justify societal permission for physicians or others to hasten the deaths of patients. In general, he contends that the institutionalization of euthanasia is so fraught with serious risks that it cannot be countenanced.

344. President's Commission for the Study of Ethical Problems in Medicine and Biomedical and Behavioral Research. Deciding to Forego Life-Sustaining Treatment: Ethical, Medical, and Legal Issues in Treatment Decisions. Washington, DC: U.S. Government Printing Office; March 1983.

This report discusses in detail the ethical implications of decision making about medical interventions near the end of life. Special considerations involved when patients lack decisionmaking capacity and when patients have permanently lost consciousness receive particular attention. The role of advance health care planning to maintain some degree of autonomy is highlighted. There is a separate chapter on resuscitation decisions. Institutional and societal constraints on decision making are laid out.

345. Price, David M.; Armstrong, Paul W. New Jersey's Granny Doe Squad: Arguments About Mechanisms for Protection of Vulnerable Patients. Law, Medicine & Health Care; Fall 1989; 17(3): 255-263.

Price and Armstrong draw a parallel between the Baby Doe debate of the early 1980s and the moral zeal to defend life for the elderly they predict is emerging in the early 1990s. As members of the New Jersey Bioethics Commission, they discuss a controversial policy (since repealed, leaving a confusing aftermath) initiated by the Office (N.J.) of the Ombudsman to examine every non-treatment decision in a nursing home as a case of possible abuse. They point to institutional ethics committees to assist in these hard situations.

346. Quill, Timothy E. Death and Dignity: A Case of Individualized Decision Making. New England Journal of Medicine; March 7, 1991; 324(10): 691-694.

Dr. Quill describes how he provided barbituates to a patient dying in severe pain of leukemia, which the patient used to commit suicide. The article makes a justification for physician-assisted suicide in certain limited circumstances.

347. Quill, Timothy E. Utilization of Nasogastric Feeding Tubes in a Group of Chronically Ill, Elderly Patients in a Community Hospital. Archives of Internal Medicine; September 1989; 149(9): 1937-1941.

Dr. Quill questions the wisdom of initiating and sustaining artificial nutritional support for patients with severe irreversible or terminal illnesses with little meaningful prospect of reversing the underlying disease and regaining nutritional independence. In a survey, he found that practicing physicians differed considerably in their belief about whether nasogastric feeding represented extraordinary, ordinary, or comfort-oriented treatment. He recommends active patient and family participation in the decision to use an NG feeding tube, requiring a fair presentation of potential benefits, burdens, and limitations for the specific patient.

348. Quinn, Kevin P. The Best Interests of Incompetent Patients: The Capacity for Interpersonal Relationships as a Standard for Decisionmaking. California Law Review; 1988; 76: 897-937.

This Comment proposes a standard for determining when life-sustaining medical treatment may be withdrawn from incompetent patients whose wishes are not known. Quinn argues that current standards used to guide surrogate decisionmaking are unsatisfactory because they fail to address the quality of life considerations that necessarily underlie any determination of whether it is worth keeping a patient alive. Making quality of life decisions requires defining the essential characteristic of being human, which the author proposes is the capacity for interpersonal relationships.

349. Rhoden, Nancy. How Should We View the Incompetent? Law, Medicine & Health Care; Fall 1989; 17(3): 264-268.

Rhoden argues for medical decisionmaking on behalf of incompetent patients, which must inevitably take into account quality of life judgments, based on a presumption for family choice, with the burden on professional caregivers to prove that the family choice impinges on the interests of a particular patient. The family should envision the patient's life as a unity, considering her prior values, whether or not such values yield definitive answers.

350. Rhoden, Nancy K. Litigating Life and Death. Harvard Law Review; 1988; 102: 375-446.

Professor Rhoden criticizes the two dominant approaches the courts have developed--the "subjective" and "objective" tests--governing termination of an incompetent patient's medical treatment and proposes that these standards be abandoned for a direct legal and ethical presumption in favor of family decisionmaking. She argues that families should be presumed to be empowered to exercise discretion over treatment choices, and should not have to meet an unreasonable burden of proof to justify limiting life-sustaining treatment.

351. Rosenblum, Victor G.; Forsythe, Clarke D. The Right to Assisted Suicide: Protection of Autonomy or an Open Door to Social Killing? Issues in Law & Medicine; Summer 1990; 6(1): 3-31.

The authors review the doctrines of autonomy and privacy as they affect the idea of assisted suicide. They argue that a right to assisted suicide would result in a fundamental and negative alteration in the physician's role, that rational suicide would defy proper regulation, that such a right would put pressure on disabled persons to decline beneficial care, and that the class of disabled persons for whom assisted suicide would be deemed appropriate would expand inexorably.

352. Rosner, Fred. Withdrawing Fluids and Nutrition: An Alternate View. New York State Journal of Medicine; November 1987; 87: 591-592.

The physician-author argues that the provision of nutrition and hydration by feeding tubes or intravenous lines is not medical treatment, but supportive care. There is a morally significant difference between supportive and medical interventions for Rosner, with the former always required regardless of the benefit/burden relationship for the particular patient.

353. Rouse, Fenalla. Does Autonomy Require Informed and Specific Refusal of Life-Sustaining Medical Treatment? Issues in Law and Medicine; Winter 1989; 5(3): 321-335.

The Director of the Society for the Right to Die answers the question posed in the article's title in the negative. The need for informed refusal, Rouse claims, does not spring from a respect for the right to be let alone, but springs instead from a societal interest in enabling a person to pursue his or her own particular plan of life and from our contemporary health care system in which we are forced to accept the idea that treatment is sometimes provided when the patient would refuse it. Allowing the family to speak for the patient in the absence of any showing of less than good intentions is more likely to promote individual choice and caring treatment of the individual than treating all patients who have not clearly expressed their wishes as identical members of a faceless class.

354. Ruark, John E.; Raffin, Thomas A.; Stanford University Medical Center Committee on Ethics. Initiating and Withdrawing Life Support: Principles and Practice in Adult Medicine. New England Journal of Medicine; January 7, 1988; 318(1): 25-30.

This document provides one ethical blueprint for decision making regarding critically ill patients. It identifies as specific principles to guide participants: establishment of the source of decisional authority; effective communication with patients and families; early determination and ongoing review of individual quality-of-life values; and recognition of patients' rights. These fundamental precepts then are applied in the contexts of initiation of basic life-support measures (food, water, supplementary oxygen), instituting advanced life-support measures (resuscitation, dialysis), withdrawing advanced life support, and withdrawal of basic life support.

355. Russ, Sheryl A. Care of the Older Person: The Ethical Challenge of American Medicine. Issues in Law & Medicine; Summer 1988; 4(1): 87-94.

A medical student rejects several proposed solutions to the challenge of providing health care to older Americans. She argues against age-based rationing of health resources by citing the remarkable variations in mental and physical conditions among older persons. She opposes euthanasia for older patients in favor of continued scientific and clinical efforts to compress morbidity by slowing the progress of incurable disease or by delaying its onset.

356. Schmitz, Phyllis. The Process of Dying With and Without Feeding and Fluids By Tube. Law, Medicine & Health Care; Spring/Summer 1991; 19(1-2): 23-26.

Based on her experience as patient care coordinator for a home care provider, the author offers a personal narrative on the process of dying by critically ill patients, including the emotional and ethical components. She suggests ways for health care professionals to appropriately participate in and contribute to the dying process.

357. Schneiderman, Lawrence J. Exile and PVS. Hastings Center Report; May/June 1990; 20(3): 5.

This article criticizes physicians for aggressively treating patients in a persistent vegetative state (PVS), likening this action to resurrecting the archaic practice of banishment or exile from human community. The author submits that withdrawing life-supporting intervention from the patient in PVS is not merely ethically permissible, but an obligatory act of beneficence.

358. Schneiderman, Lawrence J.; Spragg, Roger G. Ethical Decisions in Discontinuing Mechanical Ventilation. New England Journal of Medicine; April 14, 1988; 318(15): 984-988.

The authors present two case histories to illustrate the range of ethical issues confronted by those considering the discontinuation of mechanical ventilation. The paper proposes the following order of priority for the hierarchical defining and weighing of value considerations: medical indications, the patient's autonomy, the patient's best interests, and external factors (e.g., family feelings, institutional limits, budgetary limits). Clinical suggestions are made regarding the most appropriate way to withdraw mechanical ventilation once a decision to do so has been made.

359. Schofield, Joyce A. Care of the Older Person: The Ethical Challenge to American Medicine. Issues in Law & Medicine; Summer 1988; 4(1): 53-68.

A medical student who is president of the Christian Medical Society laments what she perceives as the current trend away from Judeo-Christian principles of dignity and worth for each person in the health care treatment of older persons. She is particularly upset about tolerance of passive euthanasia, including the withholding and withdrawing of feeding tubes from elderly patients.

360. Scofield, Giles R. Privacy (or Liberty) and Assisted Suicide. Journal of Pain and Symptom Management; July 1991; 6(5): 1-9.

Attorney Scofield argues against accepting the concept of physician-assisted suicide of mentally capable patients as a matter of social policy by changing the criminal law to condone this practice. Assisted suicide constitutes a radical transformation in medical practice and societal mores, far beyond a small addition to patient autonomy. If the goal is to eliminate individual suffering and promote privacy in the medical sphere, the author maintains, society would do better to concentrate on improving the current quality of, and access to, the health care system. Additionally we should work to ensure that decisions about life-sustaining treatment are made in a sensible and sensitive fashion, as well as improving physician/patient communication and pain management.

361. Seckler, Allison B.; Meier, Diane E.; Mulvihill, Michael; Paris, Barbara E. Substituted Judgment: How Accurate Are Proxy Predictions? Annals of Internal Medicine; July 15, 1991; 115(2): 92-98.

This study examined the factual predicate for the proposition that substituted judgment exercised for a decisionally incapacitated patient by a surrogate is the best way to protect that patient's autonomy. Using a hypothetical scenario, the authors found a relatively low degree of agreement between the wishes of patients and decisions that would be made for those patients by family members and primary care providers. Few patients had ever discussed their treatment preferences with family or physician. The article outlines some alternatives to exclusive reliance on the substituted judgment doctrine for decision making on behalf of the mentally incapacitated.

362. Shaw, Anthony. QL Revisited. Hastings Center Report; April/May 1988; 18(2): 10-12.

Dr. Shaw presents a revised version of his formula for judging the quality of life (QL) of an individual. This formula can be used to assist in moral decision making about the medical care that should be made available to the patient. The formula is presented as $ML = NE \times (H + S)$, where ML is meaningful life and NE is natural endowment, which may be enhanced by the contributions of home (H) and/or society (S). This equation is presented as a qualitative, not quantitative, contribution.

363. Sherlock, Richard; Dingus, C. Mary. Families and the Gravely Ill: Roles, Rules, and Rights. Westport, CT: Greenwood Press; 1988.

Chapter 4 analyzes, from an ethical and legal perspective, the appropriate role of family members in making medical decisions regarding critically ill loved ones. Chapter 5 discusses possible alternatives to a reliance on families as surrogate decision makers.

364. Siegler, Mark; Weisbard, Alan J. Against the Emerging Stream: Should Fluids and Nutritional Support Be Discontinued? Archives of Internal Medicine; January 1985; 145(1): 129-131.

Siegler and Weisbard express concern about the growing public and professional acceptance of the idea that it is ethically appropriate to forgo life-sustaining fluids and nutritional supports for certain classes of patients. They urge a general proscription of this practice, and give arguments why a policy of continued intervention would be beneficial to patients, individual physicians, the medical profession, and society.

365. Singer, Peter A.; Siegler, Mark. Euthanasia--A Critique. New England Journal of Medicine; June 28, 1990; 322(26): 1881-1883.

These physician authors define euthanasia as the deliberate action by a physician to terminate the life of a patient, as exemplified by a lethal injection. They criticize the main arguments made by proponents of this practice and present opposing arguments from the perspectives of public policy and traditional ethical norms of medicine. They urge physicians to become more responsive to the concerns of patients that underlie the movement for euthanasia and must provide better pain management, more compassionate terminal care, and more appropriate use of life-sustaining interventions.

366. Smedira, Nicholas G.; Evans, Bradley H.; Grais, Linda S.; et. al. Withholding and Withdrawal of Life Support From the Critically Ill. New England Journal of Medicine; February 1, 1990; 322(5): 309-315.

This study examines the ethical and psychological dynamics of the process of decisionmaking and consensus building between physicians and families regarding the limitation of life-sustaining medical interventions for mentally incapacitated patients in the intensive care unit. The authors urge attending physicians to encourage and allow more communication with, and active participation of, family members in the decisionmaking process.

367. Smith, David H.; Granbois, Judith A. The American Way of Hospice. Hastings Center Report; April 1982; 12(2): 8-10.

This article explores the ethical foundations for the hospice movement and for our attitudes toward hospice patients. Attention is paid to encouraging individual autonomy while simultaneously recognizing the patient's dependency on others.

368. Smith, George P. II. All's Well That Ends Well: Toward a Policy of Assisted Rational Suicide or Merely Enlightened Self-Determination? University of California Davis Law Review; Winter 1989; 22(2): 275-419.

This article ranges over the topics of suicide, assisted suicide, and passive euthanasia, surveying the ethical and legal landscapes in support of the author's position in support of suicide, assisted suicide, and withholding and withdrawal of life-sustaining medical interventions as exercises of an individual's fundamental right to enlightened self-determination. Governmental interests in preserving life should be promoted through voluntary means (e.g., making the existences of older persons more meaningful), not mandatory interference with personal autonomy.

369. Smith, William B. Is a Decision to Forgo Tube Feeding for Another a Decision to Kill? Issues in Law & Medicine; Spring 1991; 6(4): 385-394.

Msgr. Smith, S.T.D., analyzes the opposing presumptions and principles underlying the moral debate about artificial feeding and hydration. He argues that it is rarely permissible to forgo tube feeding for another.

370. Sprung, Charles L. Changing Attitudes and Practices in Forgoing Life-Sustaining Treatments. Journal of the American Medical Association; April 25, 1990; 263(16): 2211-2215.

Sprung contends that the seeds of active euthanasia have been firmly planted in the United States. During the past fifteen years, he writes, we have evolved from situations in which it was a deviation from the medical and ethical standard to withdraw a respirator, artificial nutrition, or intravenous fluids from a patient to the present environment, in which it is accepted practice and becoming the norm to withdraw such medical treatments in certain groups of patients. From this development, the author draws euthanasia-related parallels between the United States and contemporary Holland and nazi Germany.

371. Stanley, John M.; et. al. The Appleton Consensus: Suggested International Guidelines for Decisions to Forgo Medical Treatment. Journal of the Danish Medical Association; March 13, 1989; 151(11): 700-706.

Thirty-three delegates from ten different countries, representing medicine, law, ethics, economics, and religion, met in 1988 to produce these guidelines for treatment abatement procedures. Separate parts deal with decisions involving competent patients or patients who executed an advance directive before becoming incompetent, decisions involving patients who were once competent but are not presently competent who have not executed an advance directive, decisions involving patients who are not now and never have been competent, and the impact of resource scarcity on medical decisionmaking.

372. Steinbock, Bonnie. Recovery from Persistent Vegetative State? The

Case of Carrie Coons. Hastings Center Report; July/August 1989; 19(4): 14-15.

Using the Coons case from New York (involving an eighty-six year old woman thought to be in a persistent vegetative state) as a backdrop, philosopher Steinbock urges against the temptation to oversimplify the difficult job of medical decision making for the questionably competent by treating a patient's utterances during brief periods of consciousness as determinative.

373. Steinbock, Bonnie. The Removal of Mr. Herbert's Feeding Tube. Hastings Center Report; October 1983; 13(5): 13-16.

This article discusses the one case in American history involving a criminal prosecution against physicians for withdrawing a feeding tube from a persistently vegetative patient. Philosopher Steinbock agrees from an ethical perspective with the judge who dismissed this case prior to trial. Steinbock argues that removal of artificial sustenance from a patient in PVS is ethically appropriate, although she is unclear about extending this principle to other patient categories, like the conscious but severely demented.

374. Stone, Alan A. The Right to Die: New Problems for Law and Medicine and Psychiatry. Emory Law Journal; 1988; 37: 627-643.

Dr. Stone's thesis is that recognizing a right to refuse medical treatment leads inevitably to the right to commit suicide. There is no convincing principle, for either physicians or attorneys, to separate these two rights. While the right to die began as the ability of a terminal, vegetative patient to refuse an extraordinary, futile, invasive treatment on a machine, it has been transformed into the right of any patient to refuse any treatment and thereby force the attending physician to be complicit in suicide.

375. Streim, Joel E.; Marshall, John R. The Dying Elderly Patient. American Family Physician; November 1988; 38(5): 175-183.

Guidance is provided to primary care physicians for managing a dying older patient's final days in a manner that is ethically appropriate for physician, patient, and the family. The role of discussion and planning among the involved parties is stressed. Obstacles to optimal discussion and planning include physician reluctance to confront the reality of death, the effect of incapacitating illness on the patient's ability to participate in decisionmaking, erroneous presumptions routinely made about the decisional incapacity of older patients, a paternalistic bias toward protecting the elderly from harmful talk, and the denial of illness and impending death.

376. Task Force on Ethics of the American Society of Critical Care Medicine. Consensus Report on the Ethics of Foregoing Life-Sustaining Treatments in the Critically Ill. Critical Care Medicine; December 1990; 18(12): 1435-1439.

This is a comprehensive consensus statement of a leading medical association on the ethics of life-sustaining treatment abatement for critically ill patients. It deals with both decisionally capable and incapacitated patients, the status of feeding tubes, the role of physician/patient/family communication, surrogate decision making, and the physician's lack of obligation to provide futile medical care, among other topics.

377. Task Force on Supportive Care. The Supportive Care Plan--Its Meaning and Application: Recommendations and Guidelines. Law, Medicine & Health Care; June 1984; 12(3): 97-102.

An independent group in Minneapolis-St. Paul, Minnesota presents a set of recommendations and guidelines for the provision of supportive care (medical treatment to preserve comfort, hygiene, and dignity, but not to prolong life) to nursing home residents. This document considers the definition of supportive care, delineation of the candidates for supportive care, and establishment of procedures for initiation, review, and documentation of a supportive care plan,.

378. Teno, Joan; Lynn, Joanne. Voluntary Active Euthanasia: The Individual Case and Public Policy. Journal of the American Geriatrics Society; August 1991; 39(8): 827-830.

These authors support the position of the American Geriatrics Society in opposition to legalizing physician participation in voluntary active euthanasia. Despite some potential benefits of legalized active euthanasia, prudent public policy and good ethics requires that patient autonomy be constrained from authorizing the active hastening of one's own death. Potential adverse consequences of legalized euthanasia include abuse affecting vulnerable persons in society, patients and families driven by economic realities to choose euthanasia to escape family bankruptcy or to avoid inadequate care, changing medical practice by encouraging physicians to engage in euthanasia as easier than meticulous attention to individual symptom control and psychosocial needs, and reducing the public's trust in physicians generally.

379. Thomasma, David C. Freedom, Dependency, and the Care of the Very Old. Journal of the American Geriatrics Society; December 1984; 32(12): 906-914.

Philosopher Thomasma addresses the issue of moral guidelines for the degree of medical treatment to be given to the very old. He argues against the pure autonomy criterion and the use of quality of life judgments. As a middle ground between unbridled autonomy and paternalism for the very old, he suggests the rule of dependency, namely, that the greater the dependency of the patient on others, the greater is the care that must be taken to act to enhance his or her well-being. Well-being includes references to function, beneficence, and justice.

380. Thomasma, David C. Surrogate Decisions at Risk: The Cruzan Case. Journal of the American Geriatrics Society; May 1990; 38(5): 603-604.

Philosopher Thomasma suggests that a major change be made in the default mode of medical decision making when clinical conditions destroy the ability of patients to interact spiritually and materially in human life. Specifically, the author urges that there be a presumption in modern medicine that, absent any advance directives to the contrary, in specified states of neurological impairment, individuals will not receive medical interventions to prolong their lives.

381. Thomasma, David C. The Cruzan Decision and Medical Practice. Archives of Internal Medicine; May 1991; 151(5): 853-854.

The author suggests that much of the discussion about advance directives veers in the wrong direction, by focusing too much on the specificity of instructions rather than the default mode of modern medicine. This mode is that, absent any directives to the contrary, all individuals want everything possible done to save their lives. Thomasma urges that the default mode ought to be the reverse. It should be that, absent any directives to the contrary, in specified states of neurological impairment, individuals will not receive medical intervention (including medically delivered fluids and nutrition) to prolong their lives.

382. Thomasma, David C.; Graber, Glenn C. Euthanasia: Toward an Ethical Social Policy. New York: Continuum Publishing Company; 1990.

Although defining euthanasia very broadly, this book concentrates on passively allowing death to occur and actively hastening death in situations of terminal illness when patients are either conscious or unconscious. The authors raise the issues of unwilling and/or active death-causing, the family's perspective, the medical community's role, and the treatment of patient suffering. They argue against a public policy that would condone active euthanasia.

383. Tresch, Donald D.; Sims, Farrol H.; Duthie, Edmund H., Jr.; Goldstein, Michael D. Patients in a Persistent Vegetative State: Attitudes and Reactions of Family Members. Journal of the American Geriatrics Society; January 1991; 39(1): 17-21.

This article reports on a small survey of attitudes and reactions of family members of patients who were in a persistent vegetative state (PVS). A surprising number of these families wanted the patient to undergo aggressive therapeutic interventions to continue life, including transfer to an acute care hospital, surgery, and tube feeding.

384. Tunzi, Marc; Wollitzer, Alison O.; Blossom, John. Discussion of Code Status With Outpatients. Journal of Family Practice; 1988; 26(5): 572-573.

This study used a questionnaire to document family physician attitudes and practices regarding the discussion of resuscitation status and related end-of-life care issues with outpatients.

385. Uhlmann, Richard F.; Clark, High; Pearlman, Robert A.; Downs, Joseph C.; Addison, John H.; Haining, Robert G. Medical Management Decisions in Nursing Home Patients: Principles and Policy Recommendations. Annals of Internal Medicine; June 1987; 106(6): 879-885.

This article describes a detailed model policy developed by the King County(Washington) Medical Society to define key ethical decisionmaking principles, issues and procedures in long term care facilities. Extensive emphasis is placed on the utility of advance directives to promote patient autonomy. Model forms are included.

386. Uhlmann, Richard F.; Pearlman, Robert A. Perceived Quality of Life and Preferences for Life-Sustaining Treatment in Older Adults. Archives of Internal Medicine; March 1991; 151: 495-497.

In this study, physicians and elderly, chronically ill patients were questioned about perceived quality of life of the patient. The authors found that primary physicians generally consider their older outpatients' quality of life to be worse than do the patients. Additionally, physicians' estimates of patients' quality of life are significantly associated with physicians' attitudes toward life-sustaining treatment for the patients. For the patients, however, perceived quality of life did not seem to be associated with their preferences for life-sustaining treatment. The finding that physicians tend to underestimate their older patients' quality of life reinforces the need for caution in using such estimations in medical decision making.

387. Vaccari, Michael A. The Inability to Swallow as a Fatal Pathology. Issues in Law and Medicine; Fall 1991; 7(2): 155-167.

A central moral question is whether a patient's decision to forgo life-sustaining treatment reflects an intent to choose death or an intent to decline burdensome or ineffective treatment. In the course of this article, the author discusses the relationship between whether a patient's condition is terminal and the influence that fact has on the patient's assessment of whether a particular treatment is effective or burdensome.

388. Vaux, Kenneth L. The Theological Ethics of Euthanasia. Hastings Center Report; January/February 1989; 19(1): 19-22.

This article describes a transcendant theological ethic and explores the implications of this ethic for the issue of voluntary (active) euthanasia. Vaux examines the different types of euthanasia, the position of exceptional case euthanasia, and the question of physician participation.

389. Wanzer, Sidney H.; Federman, Daniel D.; Adelstein, S. James; et. al. The Physician's Responsibility Toward Hopelessly Ill Patients: A Second Look. New England Journal of Medicine; March 30, 1989; 320(13): 844-849.

This consensus statement by twelve prominent physicians was sponsored by the Society for the Right to Die. The statement discusses a variety of issues concerning patient rights and physician responsibilities and options concerning life-prolonging medical treatment for the critically ill. Among the topics analyzed are physician/patient communication, advance planning directives, medical education, institutional policies and procedures, pain medication usage, appropriate treatment and dying settings, and assisted suicide.

390. Watts, David T.; Cassel, Christine K. Extraordinary Nutritional Support: A Case Study and Ethical Analysis. Journal of the American Geriatrics Society; 1984; 32: 237-242.

Using a case study, the authors explain that in certain circumstances the ethical principles of autonomy and beneficence may argue for withholding or withdrawing artificial forms of sustenance.

391. Weir, Robert F. Abating Treatment with Critically Ill Patients. New York: Oxford University Press; 1989.

Philosopher Weir's panoramic view of trends related to the abatement of medical treatment (i.e., decisions not to initiate, to reduce, or to end treatment) for the critically ill reveals that we have begun to question our unthinking tendency to rely on medical technology and are moving to demedicalize dying. To aid in this process, the author offers a classification scheme for sorting out important variables in cases involving incompetent patients that takes account of such factors as the grounds for and type of incapacity, whether the patient expressed treatment preferences previously, and the availability of surrogates.

392. Wennberg, R.N. Terminal Choices: Euthanasia, Suicide, and the Right to Die. Grand Rapids, MI: William B. Erdmans Publishing Company; 1989.

This book provides a religious perspective on the moral controversies surrounding the issues of suffering, euthanasia, and suicide. The audience is both professionals and older persons and their families.

393. Wikler, Daniel. Patient Interests: Clinical Implications of Philosophical Distinctions. Journal of the American Geriatrics Society; October 1988; 36(10): 951-958.

Philosopher Wikler conceptually analyzes the concept of "best interests" in the context of making medical decisions for older patients. He concludes that, since different observers will categorize the same patient's best interests differently, the more important practical issue is who decides--whose estimate of best interests to count most--for the patient.

394. Wikler, Daniel. Not Dead, Not Dying? Ethical Categories and Persistent Vegetative State. Hastings Center Report; February/March 1988; 18(1): 41-47.

Philosopher Wikler agrees with the mounting consensus that patients in persistent vegetative state (PVS) should not be maintained on artificial life supports. However, his rationale for this position is a conceptualization of PVS as the highest functioning phase of death, rather than as the lowest functioning phase of life.

395. Williams, Mark E.; Connolly, Nancy K. What Practicing Physicians in North Carolina Rate as Their Most Challenging Geriatric Medicine Concerns. Journal of the American Geriatrics Society; November 1990; 38(11): 1230-1234.

In this survey, physicians treating older patients rated as their most difficult ethical dilemmas questions about "when to quit," "who is going to determine the use of technology," "how to help families accept no code for the hopelessly ill without feeling guilty," "Are routine ekg, sigmoidoscopy, pap smear, and mammography cost-effective at all ages," and "prolonging life where no quality exists."

396. Winslade, William J. Guarding the Exit Door: A Plea for Limited Toleration of Euthanasia. Houston Law Review; May 1988; 25: 517-524.

Although he believes that the law should not encourage physicians or others to hasten the deaths of terminally ill patients, Winslade in this article sketches a plea for limited legal toleration of active euthanasia. He suggests that in extreme situations the personal, rational choices of competent adult patients and the compassionate responses of professional caregivers or family members to hasten the patient's death should be respected. The author rejects the total prohibition of euthanasia in current law as endorsing a vitalism that disregards an honoring of individual preferences that is deeply rooted in American culture.

397. Wolf, Susan. Near Death--In the Moment of Decision. New England Journal of Medicine; 1990; 322: 208-209.

This article previews a television documentary that focuses on who should decide about life-sustaining treatment, and especially the role of patient and family. The author finds the answer to this question unclear, as is the substantive standard (patient's wishes versus objective best interests) for decisionmaking. She finds a large gap between elegant ethical theory and the reality of physician paternalistic behavior.

398. Wolf, Susan M. Holding the Line on Euthanasia. Hastings Center Report; January/February 1989; 19(1): Supp 13-15.

Wolf suggests that the consequences of legalizing active euthanasia would be unacceptable to society, because such a movement would lead to losing ground that has been gained in the realm of ethical and legal acceptance of limiting life-prolonging medical intervention for certain patients. The existing prohibition on active euthanasia has helped account for (1) the law's general willingness not to intrude on private decision making about treatment abatement, (2) an expansive reading by the courts of the right to refuse life-sustaining treatment, and (3) current attention to quality of care for dying patients.

399. Wray, Nelda; Brody, Baruch; Bayer, Timothy; et. al. Withholding Medical Treatment From the Severely Demented Patient: Decisional Processes and Cost Implications. Archives of Internal Medicine; September 1988; 148(9): 1980-1984.

This article reports on an observational study of medical decisionmaking for severely demented hospitalized patients. The authors found, among other things, that families were much more involved in decisions to withhold various forms of care than they were in decisions to give full care, i.e., aggressive medical intervention. The authors conclude that many crucial decisions regarding level of care are being made without family consultation and with considerable physician ambivalence. They recommend that hospitals develop and implement protocols for decisionmaking according to specific principles they delineate in the article. They particularly endorse a process of consultative joint medical decisionmaking in the case of a severely demented patient.

400. Yarborough, Mark. Why Physicians Must Not Give Food and Water to Every Patient. Journal of Family Practice; 1989; 29(6): 683-684.

Yarborough suggests that physicians owe a moral obligation to offer food and water to, but not to force it on, every patient. Neither is there a legal duty compelling health care providers to force-feed all people who do not eat on their own. The patient has the right to refuse the offer that the provider is required to make, and such patient refusal should be honored.

401. Youngner, Stuart J. Orchestrating a Dignified Death in the Intensive-Care Unit. Clinical Chemistry; 1990; 36(8B): 1617-1622.

As the locus of power, the critical care physician is like a conductor/composer, struggling to balance and blend various clinical, legal, moral, psychological, spiritual, and economic influences to permit patients an optimal death in less than optimal circumstances. Maintaining life as long as possible without regard to the suffering and wishes of the patient is no longer acceptable, but the alternatives involve painful judgments about the patient's desires and best interests, family sensitivities, clinical probabilities, legal risks, and benefit/burden ratios. Using case examples, Dr. Youngner examines some of these issues. He also attacks the concept of futility as a decisionmaking criteria, on the grounds of medical uncertainty and the inevitability of value judgments.

6
Institutional Ethics Committees and Ethics Consultations

402. Abramson, Marcia. Caught in the Middle: The Professional as Employee & Colleague. Generations; Winter 1985; 10(2): 35-37.

Health care professionals serving older persons frequently experience ethical tensions in carrying out their functions because of perceived conflicts between their duties to the patient, the employing institution, and professional colleagues. Abramson discusses these tensions in terms of divergent fields of practice, professional perspectives, levels of intervention, and methods of ethical reasoning. She suggests team-building activities, as well as aids to the ethical reasoning process such as institutional ethics committees, ethics rounds, and ethics consultants.

403. Annas, George J. Ethics Committees: From Ethical Comfort to Ethical Cover. Hastings Center Report; May/June 1991; 21(3): 18-21.

Annas criticizes the performance of most Institutional Ethics Committees (IECs) for behaving too much like risk management or liability control bodies. While many IECs have functioned usefully in drafting institutional policies on patient care issues with ethical overtones and in staff education, Annas believes that they are very unsuited to help with individual case consultations. He urges IECs to refocus their efforts on doing good ethics rather than institutional protection.

404. Brennan, Troyen A. Ethics Committees and Decisions to Limit Care: The Experience at the Massachusetts General Hospital. Journal of the American Medical Association; August 12, 1988; 260(6): 803-807.

The author comprehensively analyzes the 1974-86 experience of the institutional ethics committee at a major teaching hospital, drawing insights about the types of cases presented for consultation and how they were handled. Among other things, he found that patients whose cases were referred to the committee for consultation were on the whole younger than patients for whom treatment decisions were made without committee involvement.

405. Cranford, Ronald E.; Doudera, A. Edward. The Emergence of Institutional Ethics Committees. Law, Medicine & Health Care; February 1984; 12(1): 13-20.

This article describes the early development of Institutional Ethics Committees (IECs) in health care institutions. The authors delineate the potential benefits, functions, and problems of IECs in helping health care institutions to deal effectively with their difficult ethical dilemmas.

406. Fry-Revere, Sigrid. Complexities of Bioethics Require Expert Leadership. Provider; April 1989: 27-29.

This article offers a practical analysis of the pros and cons (especially the possible legal implications) of having a bioethics committee or consultant in a long term care facility. The author concludes that the advantages far outweigh any disadvantages.

407. Gibson, Joan M.; Kushner, Thomasine K. Will the Conscience of an Institution Become Society's Servant? Hastings Center Report; June 1986; 16(3): 9-11.

Two philosophers provide an overview of the accomplishments and possible future direction of Institutional Ethics Committees (IECs). While expressing a modest sense of satisfaction with present mechanisms for dealing with ethical dimensions of individual patient care decisions, the authors suggest that IECs will need to be more involved in some of the larger societal issues in the years to come. One area for greater future involvement is advocacy for the rights of incapacitated or variably capable elderly patients who are transferred from nursing homes to acute care facilities.

408. Gramelspacher, Gregory P. Institutional Ethics Committees and Case Consultation: Is There a Role? Issues in Law & Medicine; Summer 1991; 7(1): 73-82.

This article discusses the history and functions of Institutional Ethics Committees (IECs). Dr. Gramelspacher evaluates the major criticisms of IECs and emphasizes the need for self-evaluation and detailed research of their effectiveness. He suggests that IECs not become involved in case consultation until committee members seriously address the process of deliberation and agree on the means to evaluate this process.

409. Hoffman, Diane E. Does Legislating Hospital Ethics Committees Make a Difference? A Study of Hospital Ethics Committees in Maryland, the District of Columbia, and Virginia. Law, Medicine & Health Care; Spring/Summer 1991; 19(1-2): 105-119.

This study presents data collected from an extensive survey of hospital Institutional Ethics Committees (IECs) in Maryland (where IECs are mandated by statute), D.C., and Virginia. The data and the author's interpretation help to illuminate many issues about the composition and operation of IECs in practice. Special attention is focused on the roles of various IEC members, especially ethicists and attorneys.

410. Jaffe, Gregory A. Institutional Ethics Committees: Legitimate and Impartial Review of Ethical Health Care Decisions. Journal of Legal Medicine; September 1989; 10(3): 393-431.

This article outlines the history of Institutional Ethics Committees (IECs), their potential functions and responsibilities, procedural aspects of setting up and operating this mechanism, and the legal status that has been afforded these bodies. The author proposes a model for a legitimate and impartial IEC.

411. LaPuma, John; Schiedermayer, David L. Ethics Consultation: Skills, Roles, and Training. Annals of Internal Medicine; January 15, 1991; 114(2): 155-160.

This paper comprehensively discusses the role of the clinical ethics consultant, in terms of historical development, legitimacy, the relationship of the consultant to the institutional ethics committee, necessary skills, difficulties encountered, and the question of training and certification.

412. LaPuma, John; Toulmin, Stephen E. Ethics Consultants and Ethics Committees. Archives of Internal Medicine; May 1989; 149(5): 1109-1112.

The authors discuss how an ethics consultant can best participate in clinical decisionmaking in the care of individual patients in health care institutions or systems. They also explore the proper relationship between the ethics consultant and the institutional ethics committee.

413. Levine, Carol. Questions and (Some Very Tentative) Answers About Hospital Ethics Committees. Hastings Center Report; June 1984; 14(3): 9-12.

Drawing on collected experience as of 1984, this article presents basic information about Institutional Ethics Committees (IECs) in terms of definitions, functions, guidelines, benefits, disadvantages, models, membership, operation, and legal status.

414. Lynn, Joanne. Conflicts of Interest in Medical Decision-Making. Journal of the American Geriatrics Society; October 1988; 36(10): 945-950.

The current model of decision-making in medicine dictates ubiquitious conflicts of interest within the patient, the professional, between the patient and the health care delivery and financing system, among surrogate decisionmakers, and between surrogates and professionals. This article discusses the ethical implications of such conflicts, with special attention to older patients, and suggests structures for the assessment and resolution of these conflicts. Suggestions include informal human interactions managed by the primary physician, consultation with knowledgeable outsiders, group meetings, institutional ethics committees, and--as a last resort--the courts.

415. McCormick, Richard A. Ethics Committees: Promise or Peril? Law, Medicine & Health Care; September 1984; 12(4): 150-155.

In this overview, the author gives a sense of the cultural and historical conditions leading to the growing popularity of Institutional Ethics Committees

(IECs) and a brief summary of their functions and of the problems they are likely to encounter. Several recommendations are provided for making IECs more of a promise than a peril for health care institutions.

416. Moreno, Jonathan. Ethics By Committee: The Moral Authority of Consensus. Journal of Medicine & Philosophy; 1988; 13: 411.

Philosopher Moreno looks at the source of moral authority in an institutional ethics committee that operates by means of consensus. To discover this foundation, the author develops a philosophical framework for the consensus-oriented ethics committee.

417. Perkins, Henry S.; Saathoff, Bunnie S. Impact of Medical Ethics Consultations on Physicians: An Exploratory Study. American Journal of Medicine; December 1988; 85: 761-765.

The authors surveyed physicians who had requested ethics consultations at one university medical center to assess consultation impact. Responses indicated that consultations identified unrecognized ethical issues, clarified physicians' thinking, changed patient management, boosted physicians' confidence, and taught physicians a considerable amount. A supplementary medical chart review identified inappropriate family decisions for incompetent adults and the use of laboratory tests and limb restraints for terminal patients as the most frequently unrecognized ethical issues.

418. Robertson, John A. Ethics Committees in Hospitals: Alternative Structures and Responsibilities. Issues in Law & Medicine; Summer 1991; 7(1): 83-91.

Law professor Robertson discusses the origin and rationale for Institutional Ethics Committees (IECs). He analyzes the positive and negative aspects of various IEC models, the objections to IECs, and the question of whether IECs ever qualify as state actors under the principles of constitutional law. He concludes that IECs should generally be available for ethical consultation on an optional basis but that consultation should be mandatory for a narrow category of cases.

419. Siegler, Mark. Ethics Committees: Decisions By Bureaucracy. Hastings

Center Report; June 1986; 16(3): 22-24.

Dr. Siegler criticizes the development of Institutional Ethics Committees (IECs). According to him, IECs threaten to undermine the traditional physician/patient relationship and to impose new, untested administrative and regulatory burdens on patients, families, and physicians. Their existence may shift the focus of decision making from the office or bedside to the conference room or executive suite. In place of IECs, the author encourages the formation of many small advisory groups possessing great clinical expertise in their own particular specialty and composed primarily of involved clinicians but with occasional representation of other experts.

420. Siegler, Mark; Singer, Peter A. Clinical Ethics Consultation: Godsend or God Squad? American Journal of Medicine; December 1988; 85: 759-760.

The authors examine fundamental questions about what is clinical ethics, how clinical ethics relate to the standard of care, the appropriate role of clinical ethics consultation, and how clinical ethics consultation afftects physician responsibility. Siegler and Singer conclude that ethics consultation is a promising but at present incompletely evaluated mechanism of health care delivery.

421. Thompson, Mary Ann; Thompson, J. Milburn. Ethics Committees in Nursing Homes: A Qualitative Research Study. Hospital Ethics Committee Forum; 1990; 2(5): 315-327.

This study interviewed members of ethics committees in seven nonprofit nursing homes with the goal of examining the inner workings of the committees. The following concerns were addressed: the relationship between a committee's composition and its effectiveness, the changes that occur in an institution with the implementation of an ethics committee, the problems associated with ethics committee functioning, and evaluation of the committee's work.

422. Wolf, Susan M. Ethics Committees in the Courts. Hastings Center Report; June 1986; 16(3): 12-15.

This article examines the status that courts have given, and should give, to Institutional Ethics Committees (IECs) and their deliberations on individual cases.

423. Young, Patricia Ann; Pelaez, Martha. The In-Service Education Program of the Home Health Assembly of New Jersey: Ethical Education of Home-Care Providers. Generations; 1990; 14(Supplement): 37-38.

A state association representing the home care community formed an ethics committee in 1985. This article describes some of the educational activities of the committee, which may serve as a model for other professional organizations to emulate. Among the issues raised during educational programs were the ethics of mandatory reporting, short versus long-term autonomy, and the role of the home care staff in an abusive and unsafe home care environment.

424. Youngner, Stuart J.; Coulton, Claudia; Juknialis, Barbara W.; Jackson, David L. Patients' Attitudes Toward Hospital Ethics Committees. Law, Medicine & Health Care; February 1984; 12(1): 21-25.

This study is the first known attempt to determine the extent of patients' knowledge about their hospitals' institutional ethics committees (IECs), as well as their opinions regarding the general role of such committees. The patients in this study saw IECs as potentially helpful to those patients and health professionals who must grapple with difficult treatment decisions. The authors suggest that, in considering the formation and design of an IEC, each health care institution must take into account the political realities within its own environment, as well as the different needs and wishes of its patients.

425. Zweibel, Nancy R.; Cassel, Christine K. Ethics Committees in Nursing Homes: Applying the Hospital Experience. Hastings Center Report; August/September 1988; 18(4): 23-25.

This article briefly discusses the potential usefulness of Institutional Ethics Committees in nursing homes. Because of inherent characteristics of long term care institutions and their populations, both the structure (e.g., composition) and process (e.g., provisions for confidentiality) of nursing home-based IECs ordinarily will differ from that of hospital-based IECs. In nursing homes, there may be less need for individual case consultation but a greater need for IEC involvement in staff education and emotional support.

7
Resuscitation

426. American College of Emergency Physicians. Guidelines for "Do Not Resuscitate" Orders in the Prehospital Setting. Annals of Emergency Medicine; October 1988; 17(10): 1106-1108.

This document suggests principles for procedures to be developed by the appropriate Emergency Medical Services (EMS) authority for prehospital care providers to withhold cardiopulmonary resuscitation (CPR) in those patients in whom a terminal condition is known to exist. It does not attempt to set forth here substantive criteria for determining when CPR should be withdrawn or withheld from a specific person.

427. American College of Emergency Physicians, Bioethics Committee. Medical, Moral, Legal, and Ethical Aspects of Resuscitation for the Patient Who Will Have Minimal Ability to Function or Ultimately Survive. Annals of Emergency Medicine; September 1985; 14(9): 919-926.

This discussion paper regarding decision making about cardiopulmonary resuscitation proposes a strategy giving preference first to the patient's choice and, if the patient is decisionally incapacitated, next to the patient's family.

428. American Hospital Association. Effective DNR Policies: Development, Revision, Implementation. Chicago: AHA; 1990.

These guidelines review the importance of clear, practical Do Not Resuscitate policies and provide technical assistance to health care institutions in developing, revising, and implementing these protocols.

429. American Medical Association, Council on Ethical and Judicial Affairs. Guidelines for the Appropriate Use of Do-Not-Resuscitate Orders. Journal of the American Medical Association; April 10, 1991; 265(14): 1868-1871.

This AMA position statement recognizes two exceptions to the normal presumption favoring CPR. First, a patient may express in advance a preference that CPR be withheld. If the patient is incapable of expressing an autonomous preference, the decision to forgo resuscitation may be made by the patient's family or other appropriate surrogate decision maker. Second, CPR may be withheld if, in the judgment of the attending physician, an attempt to resuscitate the patient would be futile.

430. Bartholome, William G. Do Not Resuscitate Orders: Accepting Responsibility. Archives of Internal Medicine; November 1988; 148(11): 2345-2346.

This editorial suggests that we rethink the standard presumption that, in the absence of a contrary order, CPR should automatically be provided to every patient who experiences cardiac arrest. Dr. Bartholome also calls for better communication between physicians and patients about this matter. Further, he urges, health care providers, patients, and families must understand that an order not to resuscitate has no implications for any other treatment decision, that is, that a DNR order should not be allowed to contaminate other aspects of the patient's treatment.

431. Beatty, Conny D. Case of No Consent: The DNR Order As a Medical Decision. Saint Louis University Law Journal; 1987; 31: 699-727.

This Comment suggests that the informed consent doctrine is inappropriate when applied to resuscitation decisions for irreversible and terminally ill patients. Specifically, the author argues that physicians are at some point more qualified than patients to determine when to attempt CPR. The distinction between medical expertise and the patient's personal autonomy hinges on the patient's prognosis, rather than on any quality-of-life assessment.

432. Blackhall, Leslie J. Must We Always Use CPR? New England Journal of Medicine; November 12, 1987; 317(20): 1281-1285.

This article presents a case in which the patient and family made a decision in favor of resuscitation that ran contrary to the physician's medical judgment. The author argues that, where a patient's request for treatment is in conflict with a physician's responsibility to provide what he or she believes to be good medical care, a resort to patient autonomy alone is insufficient. The principle of autonomy, which allows patients to refuse any procedure or choose among different beneficial treatments, does not allow them to demand nonbeneficial and potentially harmful procedures. CPR should not even have been considered an alternative to be offered by the physician here. Instead, the physician should have listened to the patient's hopes and fears, reassured him that the physicians would continue to be there and provide appropriate therapy, and, if necessary, refer the patient to psychiatric personnel or clergy.

433. Brennan, Troyen A. Do-Not-Resuscitate Orders for the Incompetent Patient in the Absence of Family Consent. Law, Medicine & Health Care; 1986; 14(1): 13-19.

The author provides a case report based on personal experience in which the medical team was forced to grapple with the ethical implications of issuing a Do Not Resuscitate (DNR) order for a decisionally incapacitated patient over the family's objections. The role of the Institutional Ethics Committee (IEC) in the decisionmaking process is discussed. Brennan analyzes this case in terms of a physician duty-based ethics, but finds that ethical theories can only provide the parameters or boundaries that the physician must integrate and apply to reach specific medical decisions.

434. Brunetti, Louis L.; Carperos, Stephanie D.; Westlund, Ronald E. Physicians' Attitudes Towards Living Wills and Cardiopulmonary Resuscitation. Journal of General Internal Medicine; July/August 1991; 6(4): 323-329.

This survey of North Carolina physicians found that, while most of them were aware of the living will as a mechanism available for advance health care planning, and while most of them would wish to forgo cardiopulmonary resuscitation themselves in certain situations, these physicians generally were reluctant to initiate conversations with their patients about medical decision making and treatment preferences. Physicians are admonished to do a better job of bringing their daily practices, including office-based patient care, more into line with their beliefs about life-sustaining treatment and advance planning.

435. Brunetti, Louis L.; Weiss, Matthew J.; Studenski, Stephanie A.; Clipp, Elizabeth C. Cardiopulmonary Resuscitation Policies and Practices: A Statewide Nursing Home Study. Archives of Internal Medicine; January 1990; 150(1): 121-126.

The authors compared the content of written resuscitation policies of North Carolina nursing homes to ten model criteria regarded as important to the decisionmaking process: autonomy, informed consent, competency, dignity and quality of life, treatment alternatives, authorization, documentation, patient identification, review, and medical condition. They found that nursing home policies were most likely to contain provisions that could be objectively measured and easily documented and were required by law. They suggest that inclusion of their ten study criteria would help enhance autonomy and the quality of decision making by nursing home residents.

436. Cassel, Christine K. Ethical Issues in the Emergency Care of Elderly Persons: A Framework for Decision Making. Mount Sinai Journal of Medicine; January 1987; 54(1): 9-13.

Dr. Cassel discusses a range of ethical issues concerning elderly people in emergency department situations. Using the three key principles of beneficence (including non-maleficence), respect for persons, and justice, she shows that there is a systematic way of thinking about ethical problems arising in the care of older patients. Since the focus here is on emergency decision making, resuscitation issues are put forward as the main example.

437. Emanuel, Linda L. Does the DNR Order Need Life-Sustaining Intervention? Time for Comprehensive Advance Directives. American Journal of Medicine; January 1989; 86: 87-90.

There are a wide range of life-sustaining medical interventions that might be deemed inappropriate by patients and their families at times. It is argued here that we must subsume the resuscitation decision into comprehensive and timely health care directives. Different approaches to early, comprehensive directives including but not limited to Do Not Resuscitate orders are outlined, and a case report is presented that illustrates one of the approaches--discussion with patient and family during an office visit.

438. Enck, Robert E.; Longa, Daniel R.; Warren, Matthew; McCann, Barbara A. DNR Policies in Healthcare Organizations With Emphasis on Hospice. American Journal of Hospice Care; November/December 1988: 39-42.

Based on a 1986 survey conducted by the JCAHO, this article discusses the prevalence and importance of formal resuscitation policies in hospices, as well as some of the common problems encountered in implementing Do Not Resuscitate policies in the hospice setting.

439. Gleeson, Kevin; Wise, Scott. The Do-Not-Resuscitate Order: Still Too Little Too Late. Archives of Internal Medicine; May 1990; 150(5): 1057-1060.

This study found that a Do Not Resuscitate (DNR) order is usually written preceding the death of chronically ill hospitalized individuals. Although the percentage of patients involved in the decision to limit intervention seems to be increasing, the majority of these patients remain uninvolved in this decision. The authors argue that, in accord with prevailing ethical principles, early and intensive efforts to involve patients in decisions concerning their terminal care are warranted.

440. Hackler, J. Chris; Hiller, F. Charles. Family Consent to Orders Not to Resuscitate: Reconsidering Hospital Policy. Journal of the American Medical Association; September 12, 1990; 264(10): 1281-1283.

These authors propose that a physician should not be required to offer cardiopulmonary resuscitation to patients or families where, in the physician's professional judgment, the intervention would be futile. Hackler and Hiller also propose that CPR be withheld, even over family objections, where (1) the patient personally lacks decisionmaking capacity, (2) the burdens of treatment are disproportionate to the benefits, (3) the surrogate cannot justify CPR in terms of patient values, preferences, or best interests, and (4) the physician has made serious efforts to negotiate and resolve the issue informally with the family. The authors opine that the legal risks to the physician of acting on their consciences even over family objections are very slight.

441. Havlir, Diane; Brown, Louise; Rousseau, G. Kay. Do Not Resuscitate

Discussions in a Hospital-Based Home Care Program. Journal of the American Geriatrics Society; January 1989; 37(1): 52-54.

This pilot study demonstrates the feasibility, indeed the desirability, of discussing CPR code status with seriously ill, elderly patients and/or their families in the outpatient setting of a hospital-based home care program. The patients and families welcomed the opportunity to discuss code status with the providers. Benefits of these discussions are outlined.

442. Jonsson, Palmi V.; McNamee, Michael; Campion, Edward W. The Do Not Resuscitate Order: A Profile of Its Changing Use. Archives of Internal Medicine; November 1988; 148(11): 2373-2375.

From a study of deaths in a community hospital, the authors conclude that explicit DNR orders are now the rule rather than the exception, but that resuscitation decisions usually are made late and involve family members much more than the patient. They also discuss the irrelevance of the DNR order to the intensity of other forms of care. They urge that, regardless of the patient's age, a DNR order should reflect the prognosis of illness or recovery and the wishes of patient and family.

443. LaPuma, John; Silverstein, Marc D.; Stocking, Carol B.; Roland, Dianne; Siegler, Mark. Life-Sustaining Treatment: A Prospective Study of Patients With DNR Orders in a Teaching Hospital. Archives of Internal Medicine; October 1988; 148(10): 2193-2198.

This article reports on a prospective study of attending and postgraduate trainee physicians who had written a Do Not Resuscitate (DNR) order for patients in their care. The authors conclude that individual physicians interpret the meaning of the DNR order very differently, in terms of specific life-sustaining medical interventions to be withheld or withdrawn from a patient. They found that, in practice, physicians draw a strong distinction between not initiating an intervention, on one hand, versus discontinuing an intervention already in place, on the other.

444. Lehman, Lawrence B. Do Not Resuscitate. Resident & Staff Physician; August 1989; 35(9): 69-72.

Dr. Lehman urges physicians to discuss resuscitation status with patients in a timely and open manner, before a crisis has unfolded. The patient's medical condition and prognosis are of prime importance. Also fundamental to all DNR conversations is the understanding that this designation refers only to resuscitative efforts should cardiopulmonary arrest occur, and is not synonymous with a decision to defer aggressive treatment of other primary or secondary medical conditions.

445. Leivers, David. Letter, Questions About DNR Orders. Journal of the American Medical Association; August 14, 1991; 266(6): 795.

This letter raises ethical issues that surround resuscitation decisions and Do Not Resuscitate orders in the operating room, particularly in patients undergoing palliative surgery. The author addresses these questions from the perspective of the anesthesiologist.

446. Miles, Steven H.; Crimmins, Timothy J. Orders to Limit Emergency Treatment for an Ambulance Service in a Large Metropolitan Area. Journal of the American Medical Association; July 26, 1985; 254: 525-527.

The authors describe a program for nursing home residents and their physicians to document in their medical records Do Not Resuscitate (DNR) and Do Not Intubate (DNI) orders for emergency care by pre-hospital personnel.

447. Miller, Tracy E. Do-Not-Resuscitate Orders: Public Policy and Patient Autonomy. Law, Medicine & Health Care; Fall 1989; 17(3): 245-254.

The Director of the New York State Task force on Life and the Law describes the confusion and concerns surrounding the use of Do Not Resuscitate (DNR) orders that led to the Task Force's involvement and its choice of a legislative response. She then discusses the Task Force's recommendations, focusing on policies that delineate the role of competent patients and the determination of decisional capacity. Some preliminary observations about how these proposals, enacted legislatively in 1987, have fared in practice are set forth.

448. Moss, Alvin H. Informing the Patient About Cardiopulmonary Resuscitation: When the Risks Outweigh the Benefits. Journal of General

Internal Medicine; July/August 1989; 4(4): 349-355.

The author reviews extensive literature documenting very poor results for patients receiving cardiopulmonary resuscitation, in terms of survival and recovery. He argues that physicians have an obligation to educate patients and their families accurately about the risks and benefits of treatment alternatives, to maximize their informed participation in treatment decisionmaking. He also comments on resolving differences where the patient or family insist upon remaining eligible to receive CPR despite the physician's judgment that such intervention would be medically futile.

449. Murphy, Donald J.; Murray, Anne M.; Robinson, Bruce E.; Campion, Edward W. Outcomes of Cardiopulmonary Resuscitation in the Elderly. Annals of Internal Medicine; August 1, 1989; 111(3): 199-205.

This study concludes that elderly patients and their families have a right to know the truth about the statistically poor outcomes of cardiopulmonary resuscitation (CPR). Knowing the grim facts may make a Do Not Resuscitate (DNR) decision much less difficult for patient, family, and the medical team. Physicians should be aware of the facts and use them to make more judicious decisions about subjecting sick older patients to CPR attempts.

450. Neher, Jon O. The Slow Code: A Hidden Conflict. Journal of Family Practice; 1988; 27(4): 429-430.

This article discusses the definition of a "slow code" for half-hearted cardiopulmonary resuscitation, the reasons that physicians (usually medical residents) feel the need to resort to "slow codes," ethical objections to this practice, and what steps can be taken to reduce their use. Primary strategies are documentation of patient and family wishes in a timely fashion and better overall communication techniques.

451. Podrid, Philip J. Resuscitation in the Elderly: A Blessing or a Curse? Annals of Internal Medicine; August 1, 1989; 111(3): 193-195.

This editorial comments on research regarding the general ineffectiveness of cardiopulmonary resuscitation (CPR) for many elderly persons. In light of these findings, the author suggests that it may be time to establish meaningful guidelines for Do Not Resuscitate (DNR) orders in elderly hospitalized patients in order to spare them costly, artificial, and uncomfortable measures that only serve to delay death. Frank and open discussion of this difficult and emotional issue is required between medical providers and the patient and family.

452. Rahman, Fazlur. No CPR, Please. Senior Patient; September/October 1989; 1(5): 89-92.

An oncologist implores fellow physicians to acknowledge that routine resuscitation of every older patient in a life-threatening situation is not good clinical or ethical practice where CPR is likely only to prolong the dying process. He discusses the need for better communication among physician, patient, and family on this issue and clearer documentation by competent patients concerning future treatment preferences.

453. Ross, Judith W.; Pugh, Deborah. Limited Cardiopulmonary Resuscitation: The Ethics of Partial Codes. Quality Review Bulletin; January 1988; 14(1): 4-8.

This article discusses the ethical acceptability of limited or partial codes, defined here as situations in which a patient receives some, but not all, of the discrete elements of cardiopulmonary resuscitation (CPR). This situation occurs as a result of a prior decision, stated in a written or verbal order by the patient's physician, either to omit specific elements of CPR or to provide only certain elements of CPR. Partial codes may be motivated and justified by considerations of autonomy or beneficence. Where a partial code intends to deceive the patient and family, however, it usually cannot be justified ethically.

454. Sachs, Greg A.; Miles, Steven H.; Levin, Rebekah A. Limiting Resuscitation: Emerging Policy in the Emergency Medical System. Annals of Internal Medicine; January 15, 1991; 114(2): 151-154.

This article describes the results of a nationwide telephone survey of state offices for coordination of emergency medical services (EMS) to see how the states deal with the potential conflict between paramedics' standing orders to provide cardiopulmonary resuscitation whenever it is medically indicated and the wishes of certain patients and families to forgo CPR where it will only postpone death. State and local policies on prehospital Do Not Resuscitate decisions are summarized. This issue is especially relevant to the care of older persons who are receiving care in community settings when the EMS agency is called.

455. Schade; Muslin. Do Not Resuscitate Decisions: Discussions With Patients. Journal of Medical Ethics; 1989; 15: 186-187.

These authors propose that not all patients be informed of their resuscitation status, that information about such status be communicated over time, and that sharing further information be governed by the patient's response to previous information. The physician has a duty to discover the extent, if any, to which the individual patient wishes to participate in DNR decisionmaking.

456. Shaver, Elizabeth. Do Not Resuscitate: The Failure to Protect the Incompetent Patient's Right of Self-Determination. Cornell Law Review; 1989; 75(1): 218-245.

This Note analyzes New York's statute that allows a physician to issue a Do Not Resuscitate (DNR) order for an incompetent patient without a surrogate if two physicians concur that resuscitation would be medically futile. The author contends that this provision does not adequately protect the right of self-determination of the incompetent patient without a surrogate because the physician issuing the order cannot possibly know the important, non-medical factors involved in making an irreversible treatment decision. In these situations, a hospital ethics committee together with a guardian ad litem can best protect the incompetent patient's interests.

457. Starr, T. Jolene; Pearlman, Robert A.; Uhlmann, Richard F. Quality of Life and Resuscitation Decisions in Elderly Patients. Journal of General Internal Medicine; November/December 1986; 1(6): 373-379.

The authors studied the assessments of elderly inpatients and their attending physicians concerning patient quality of care and resuscitation decisions for the patients' current health situation and for two hypothetical scenarios. The physicians tended to rate quality of life lower and to favor resuscitation less frequently than did their patients, for both the actual and hypothetical patients. Since assessments of quality of life may be an important determinant of physician conduct regarding such matters as CPR, differences in assessment have important implications for patient autonomy.

458. Stolman, Cynthia J.; Gregory, John J.; Dunn, Dorothea; Levine, Jeffrey L. Evaluation of Patient, Physician, Nurse, and Family Attitudes Toward Do Not Resuscitate Orders. Archives of Internal Medicine; March 1990; 150(3): 653-658.

These authors conclude their report on a survey of attitudes toward cardiopulmonary resuscitation with the recommendation that physicians introduce the topic of resuscitation early in the physician/patient relationship before hospitalization and diminished decisional capacity occur, so that a dialogue is started at a time when the patient can consider the issues rationally and discuss them fully with family members or close friends.

459. Tomlinson, Tom; Brody, Howard. Ethics and Communication in Do-Not-Resuscitate Orders. New England Journal of Medicine; January 7, 1988; 318(1): 43-46.

The authors identify the three distinct rationales for Do Not Resuscitate (DNR) orders as: no medical benefit, poor quality of life after cardiopulmonary resuscitation (CPR), and poor quality of life before CPR. They contrast these three rationales in terms of the relevance of the patient's values and the generalizability of CPR to other treatments. Tomlinson and Brody then show how distinctions among the three rationales for DNR orders make a difference for communication with patients and families, for communication among health professionals, and for institutional policies.

460. Ventres, William; Nichter, Mark. Letter, Questions About DNR Orders. Journal of the American Medical Association; August 14, 1991; 266(6): 794-795.

This letter suggests that, not only should physicians discuss Do Not Resuscitate orders with hospitalized patients and note DNR decisions openly, but physicians also should investigate and acknowledge the meanings that patients and families both hold about resuscitative efforts and a good death.

461. Wachter, Robert M.; Luce, John M.; Hearst, Norman; Lo, Bernard. Decisions About Resuscitation: Inequities Among Patients With Different

Diseases But Similar Prognoses. Annals of Internal Medicine; September 15, 1989; 111(6): 525-532.

This study found that, after adjusting for potential confounding variables and in spite of comparability of prognoses, physicians were more likely to write do not resuscitate orders for patients with AIDS or lung cancer than for patients with cirrhosis or congestive heart failure. The authors argue that this practice is unfair, and should be remedied by more discussion between physicians and patients about preferences concerning life-sustaining medical interventions like CPR.

462. Wetle, Terrie; Levkoff, Sue; Cwikel, Julie; Rosen, Amy. Nursing Home Resident Participation in Medical Decisions: Perceptions and Preferences. Gerontologist; June 1988; 28(Supplement): 32-38.

Researchers surveyed residents of nine nursing homes regarding their perceptions of and preferences for personal participation in resuscitation decisions. The residents varied greatly in both perceptions and preferences. Nurses who were surveyed consistently underestimated the amount and adequacy of information the residents were given. Ethical and practical implications of these findings are discussed.

463. Youngner, Stuart J. Do-Not-Resuscitate Orders: No Longer Secret, But Still a Problem. Hastings Center Report; February 1987; 17(1): 24-33.

This article praises hospitals for establishing formal policies for making and recording Do Not Resuscitate (DNR) decisions prudently, fairly, and humanely. However, many other kinds of decisions concerning other sorts of interventions need to be made every day in the context of critical care, and Youngner urges health care facilities to develop explicit ethical guidelines concerning these other aspects of medical treatment.

464. Zorowitz, Robert A. An Additional Letter on CPR in Nursing Homes. Journal of the American Geriatrics Society; October 1990; 38(10): 1161-1162.

The author argues that the physician has a moral obligation to discuss CPR options with his or her nursing home patients, as well as other treatment or non-treatment options. The physician should take the initiative in discussing various treatment modalities to preserve the patient's autonomy both within the nursing home and in the event that the patient at some point is transferred to another facility.

8
Futile Medical Treatment

465. Ackerman, Felicia. The Significance of a Wish. Hastings Center Report; July/August 1991; 21(4): 27-29.

Philosopher Ackerman argues that physicians have no ethical right to refuse to provide life-prolonging medical interventions requested by a patient or the patient's family on the grounds that those interventions would be futile. The question of futility and therefore of appropriateness, she maintains, is one of ethical values rather than scientific expertise. Hence, the values of the patient or family ought to prevail as a matter of decisional autonomy. Cost implications are ethically irrelevant.

466. Brennan, Troyen A. Incompetent Patients With Limited Care in the Absence of Family Consent: A Study of Socioeconomic and Clinical Variables. Annals of Internal Medicine; November 15, 1988; 109: 819-825.

The author looks at factors influencing physician entry of Do Not Resuscitate (DNR) orders for incompetent patients against the wishes of the patient's families. He speculates that this event happens fairly infrequently. Brennan concludes that, when physicians write DNR orders despite a family's request that an incompetent, terminally ill patient be resuscitated, they usually are not breaching a moral boundary on which the concept of limited care has been based in the past. He cites the experience of the Optimum Care Committee to suggest that an institutional ethics committee can play a valuable role as a consultant when further medical care seems futile but the family persists.

467. Brett, Allan S.; McCullough, Laurence B. When Patients Request Specific Interventions: Defining the Limits of the Physician's Obligation. New England Journal of Medicine; November 20, 1986; 315(21): 1347-1351.

This article discusses a patient's positive or affirmative right to a specific requested intervention in the context of the physician/patient relationship. The concern here is with the extent to which an individual patient within the health care system is entitled to a specific diagnostic or therapeutic intervention of his or her own choosing. When the patient's request conflicts with the physician's conception of acceptable medical practice, the authors argue that the ethical principles of autonomy and beneficence do not compel the physician to practice bad medicine by providing non-beneficial services.

468. Callahan, Daniel. Medical Futility, Medical Necessity: The Problem Without a Name. Hastings Center Report; July/August 1991; 21(4): 30-35.

In this essay, Callahan explores the parallel issues of defining medical futility and medical necessity. For both issues, a key is the separation of medical (factual) from moral (normative) judgment. If a consensus could be reached on what medical services were minimally necessary, the foundation could be laid for universal health care. If the same could be done for medical futility, we might then have a way to set some reasonable boundaries to such health care, useful for the purposes of individual patient welfare and societal resources.

469. Carlon, Graziano C. Just Say No. Critical Care Medicine; January 1989; 17(1): 106-107.

The author argues that, given today's economic realities, a certain amount of rationing of expensive medical treatment is inevitable and ought to be done explicitly. In this unsettling climate, one positive ethical thing that critical care physicians can do is to identify when continued aggressive treatment for a particular patient has reached the point of futility, and to have the courage to discontinue aggressive intervention at that point both to avoid unnecessary suffering and to conserve scarce resources.

470. Faber-Langendoen, Kathy. Resuscitation of Patients With Metastatic Cancer: Is Transient Benefit Still Futile? Archives of Internal Medicine; February 1991; 151(2): 235-239.

This article reviews the changing use of cardiopulmonary resuscitation (CPR) since its introduction, presents the available data on the outcome of CPR with metastatic cancer, and examines whether, in light of these data, offering CPR to patients with cancer is consonant with the goals of medicine. The physician-author concludes that offering CPR to such patients, or to following the demands of such patients for CPR, is not consistent with the chief goal of reducing suffering.

471. Jecker, Nancy S. Knowing When to Stop: The Limits of Medicine. Hasting Center Report; May/June 1991; 21(3): 5-8.

This historical analysis argues for a return in medicine from the current attitude that science can and should solve all problems to the Hippocratic tradition that teaches both physicians and patients to acknowledge and abide by limits. Under the latter tradition, physicians are not ethically required to provide, nor are patients and families entitled to insist on receiving, medically futile treatment.

472. Lantos, John D.; Singer, Peter A.; Walker, Robert M.; Gramelspacher, Gregory P.; Shapiro, Gary R.; Sanchez-Gonzalez, Miguel, A.; Stocking, Carol B.; Miles, Stephen H.; Siegler, Mark. The Illusion of Futility in Clinical Practice. American Journal of Medicine; July 1989; 87: 81-84.

The claim that a treatment is futile has serious ethical consequences for physicians and patients, in terms of justifying unilateral physician decisions to withhold or withdraw therapy. It is generally held that patients have no right to demand futile intervention over the physician's objection. This article argues that, despite the far reaching consequences of the concept, there is little consensus about how futility should be determined in practice. The authors examine the use of futility in ethics, public policy, and law, and identify current ambiguities. They contend that, because futility cannot be defined precisely, but is simply the end of a spectrum of low-efficacy therapies, the futility claim should not justify a radical shift in ethical obligations.

473. Marsh, Frank H.; Staver, Allen. Physician Authority for Unilateral DNR Orders. Journal of Legal Medicine; June 1991; 12(2): 115-165.

This article is concerned with the medical decisionmaking process and the extent to which an individual is entitled to request administration of cardiopulmonary resuscitation (CPR). The physician/patient relationship is examined with emphasis on the obligations and rights of the respective parties and the manner in which these obligations and rights are affected or otherwise qualified by the physician's assessment of the patient's condition. The authors argue that a patient does not have an ethical or a legal right to demand futile intervention.

474. Miles, Steven H. Futile Feeding at the End of Life: Family Virtues and Treatment Decisions. Theoretical Medicine; 1987; 8(3): 293-302.

Dying patients must be viewed not merely as autonomous beings isolated from all others, but rather as participants embedded in family relationships. From this perspective, Dr. Miles gives physicians a new ethical framework for analyzing and acting upon family requests for artificial feeding for a dying loved one.

475. Miles, Steven H. Informed Demand for Non-Beneficial Medical Treatment. New England Journal of Medicine; August 15, 1991; 325(7): 512-515.

A physician describes the ethical reasoning that led one hospital to seek a court order permitting it to discontinue providing aggressive medical treatment to a patient whom the hospital believed was no longer capable of benefiting from that treatment. This court order was sought over the objections of the family, which was representing the presumed wishes of the patient.

476. Murphy, Donald J.; Matchar, David B. Life-Sustaining Therapy: A Model for Appropriate Use. Journal of the American Medical Association; October 24/31, 1990; 264(16): 2103-2108.

The authors propose a model for determining when the provision of life-sustaining medical care to a patient is ethically inappropriate because it is futile. Their operational definition of futility incorporates several different factors, including patient preferences and the principle of stewardship of scarce resources.

477. Ramos, Theodore; Reagan, James E. 'No' When the Family Says 'Go': Resisting Families' Requests for Futile CPR. Annals of Emergency Medicine; August 1989; 18(8): 898-899.

The authors argue that ethical physicians should withhold cardiopulmonary resuscitation, even where the family demands it, when the physicians judge CPR futile for prolonging life and restoring health to patients with severe cardiopulmonary-cerebral insults. Health care institutions should have clear guidelines in this area to support clinicians.

478. Rie, Michael A. The Limits of a Wish. Hastings Center Report; July/August 1991; 21(4): 24-27.

Dr. Rie discusses the case of Helga Wanglie, an elderly woman in a persistent vegetative state whose family insisted on maximal life-sustaining medical treatment (e.g., respirator, feeding tubes) even though the medical staff thought such treatment was futile. Dr. Rie argues that the physicians, as moral agents participating in a trust relationship with the patient, have a moral right to refuse to provide what they believe to be futile medical interventions, and that patients and families do not have the moral right, under the umbrella of autonomy, to demand that physicians violate their own ethical integrity to provide such treatment.

479. Schneiderman, Lawrence J.; Jecker, Nancy S.; Jonsen, Albert R. Medical Futility: Its Meaning and Ethical Implications. Annals of Internal Medicine; June 15, 1990; 112(12): 949-954.

These authors distinguish between medical futility in a quantitative and a qualitative sense. Quantitatively, it refers to an expectation of success that is either predictably or empirically so unlikely that its exact probability is often incalculable. Qualitatively, it refers to any treatment that merely preserves permanent unconsciousness or that fails to end total dependence on intensive medical care. In their judgment, it is not necessary for physicians to let patients decide on treatment if it is either quantitatively or qualitatively futile.

480. Tomlinson, Tom; Brody, Howard. Futility and the Ethics of Resuscitation. Journal of the American Medical Association; September 12, 1990; 264(10): 1276-1280.

These authors propose a social mechanism to achieve mutually agreed-upon standards regarding the futility of resuscitation attempts; this is not a situation where physicians should impose their own values (even if reasonable) on the worth of CPR on patients. Both physician and patient integrity would be served by the joint development of general social standards to make the necessary value judgments about which treatments may be withheld without individual discussion between physician and patient or family.

481. Yarborough, Mark. Continued Treatment of the Fatally Ill for the Benefit of Others. Journal of the American Geriatrics Society; January 1988; 36(1): 63-67.

A philosopher discusses the question of continuing medical treatment (such as intubation) for a patient who is incapable of benefiting in order to serve the emotional and psychological needs of a third party such as a spouse or child. He finds that, while such a practice might be morally justifiable in some instances in terms of treating persons with dignity and respect, it almost always will constitute poor professional medical practice.

482. Youngner, Stuart J. Who Defines Futility? Journal of the American Medical Association; October 14, 1988; 260(14): 2094-2095.

This commentary quarrels with those who argue that a physician has no duty to provide or even offer medical interventions that he or she deems to be futile for a specific patient. The author points out that the concept of medical futility may be examined in many different ways, in terms of physiology, postponing death, length of life, quality of life, and probabilities. Other than physiological or survival futility, the other aspects of this concept all involve value judgments and physicians run the risk of giving opinions disguised as data. Until there are clear societal rules on this point, Dr. Youngner argues that information and decisions about medical interventions should be presented to patients and families, rather than withholding choices from them on grounds of perceived futility by the physician.

9

Advance Health Care Planning
and Treatment Directives

483. Brett, Allan S. Limitations of Listing Specific Medical Interventions in Advance Directives. Journal of the American Medical Association; August 14, 1991; 266(6): 825-828.

Dr. Brett suggests that a checklist of specific medical interventions to be provided or withheld under specific scenarios is not a useful component of an advance directive. The focus on specific procedures may divert attention inappropriately away from the patient's treatment goals, does not necessarily enhance self-determination, and may supply a false sense of certainty. This conclusion does not preclude asking open-ended questions to elicit patient preferences for or against specific therapies. It also does not preclude the patient's execution of a proxy directive naming an agent to make future decisions. In the final analysis, the most important element in planning for mental incapacity is the quality of communication among patients, families, and health care providers.

484. Cantor, Norman L. My Annotated Living Will. Law, Medicine & Health Care; Spring-Summer 1990; 18(1-2): 114-122.

The author, a law school professor, presents his personalized advance health care directive, complete with annotations. He offers this document for two reasons. First, by addressing various medical conditions and issues, it may encourage other people to consider a full spectrum of situations in advance and thus to provide better guidance than is currently offerred im many abbreviated living will forms. Second, to the extent that persons adopt positions close to the instructions given here, they will be reinforcing one conception of what constitutes humane treatment for a previously vigorous adult who faces a life-threatening illness or condition.

485. Davidson, Kent W.; Hackler, Chris; Caradine, Delbra R.; McCord, Ronald S. Physicians' Attitudes on Advance Directives. Journal of the American Medical Association; November 3, 1989; 262(17): 2415-2419.

This study surveys Arkansas physicians' opinions and experiences with advance directives (i.e., living wills and durable powers of attorney), as well as the reactions of patients and families to discussing the topic of advance health care planning. The investigators found an impressive depth and extent of physician support for advance planning devices, based largely on professed commitment to patient autonomy. Many physicians who had used advance directives to aid in decisionmaking in critical situations were strong proponents of the desirability of involving the patient and/or family in advance planning and documentation.

486. Diamond, Eric L.; Jernigan, James A.; Moseley, Ray A.; Messina, Valerie; McKeown, Robert A. Decision-Making Ability and Advance Directive Preferences in Nursing Home Patients and Proxies. Gerontologist; October 1989; 29(5): 622-626.

These investigators surveyed a small number of nursing home residents and their proxy decision makers to assess decisional capacity and their preferences regarding advance directives (specifically, living wills). Most patients willingly stated preferences, with the majority (especially of those determined to possess decisional capacity) desiring to avoid excessively burdensome medical treatment. The disapproval of life-sustaining interventions was even stronger among the proxy group.

487. Doukas, David J.; McCullough, Laurence B. The Values History: The Evaluation of the Patient's Values and Advance Directives. Journal of Family Practice; 1991; 32(2): 145-153.

The authors propose their Values History as a tool to enhance the patient's autonomy by clarifying and documenting for the health care team and the family the patient's expressed values underlying decisions to be carried out when decision making by the patient is no longer possible. The instrument is attached as an Appendix to the article.

488. Emanuel, Ezekiel J.; Emanuel, Linda L. Living Wills: Past, Present, and Future. Journal of Clinical Ethics; 1990; 1(1): 9-19.

The authors discuss the ethical and legal implications of advance directives such as living wills and durable powers of attorney to indicate a patient's future medical treatment preferences. They offer advance directive models that would allow patients to specify their treatment wishes with more particularity than is permitted with the documents most commonly used today.

489. Emanuel, Linda L. Does the DNR Order Need Life-Sustaining Intervention?   Time for Comprehensive Advance Directives. American Journal of Medicine; January 1989; 86: 87-90.

There are a wide range of life-sustaining medical interventions that might be deemed inappropriate by patients and their families at times. It is argued here that we must subsume the resuscitation decision into comprehensive and timely health care directives. Different approaches to early, comprehensive directives including but not limited to Do Not Resuscitate orders are outlined, and a case report is presented that illustrates one of the approaches--discussion with patient and family during an office visit.

490. Emanuel, Linda L.; Barry, Michael J.; Stoeckle, John D.; Ettelson, Lucy M.; Emanuel, Ezekiel J. Advance Directives for Medical Care--A Case for Greater Use. New England Journal of Medicine; March 28, 1991; 324(13): 889-895.

A survey of outpatients and members of the Boston public indicated that the vast majority were favorably inclined toward advance planning for medical care.   Preferences regarding interventions could not be inferred from a patient's age, health, or other demographic features.   The barriers to planning, as perceived by patients, could be substantially overcome by physicians initiating the discussion. The authors argue for a medical ethos of personal care tailored to the individual patient and an emphasis on the use of advance directives for a broad population.

491. Gamble, Elizabeth R.; McDonald, Penelope J.; Lichstein, Peter R. Knowledge, Attitudes, and Behavior of Elderly Persons Regarding Living Wills. Archives of Internal Medicine; February 1991; 151(2): 277-280.

This study indicates that many elderly patients want to share planning for terminal illness with their physicians but have never demanded or been given the opportunity. The authors suggest that physicians take a more active role in promoting discussions of patient wishes regarding end-of-life care and in informing patients and their families of options for advance directives. Open communication remains the cornerstone for ensuring patient autonomy and participation.

492. Gibson, Joan M. National Values History Project. Generations; 1990; 14(Supplement): 51-64.

There is a need for a practical mechanism (including both process and document) to assist people in articulating and recording their medical treatment preferences, values, and choices ahead of time. From a "values inventory form," first developed by volunteer medical treatment guardians as a way to reconstruct a profile or "voice" for their decisionally incapacitated wards, grew a National Values History Project. This article describes the project and reprints the Values History Form.

493. Goldstein, Mary K.; Vallone, Robert P.; Pascoe, Dennis C.; Winograd, Carol H. Durable Power of Attorney for Health Care: Are We Ready for It? Western Journal of Medicine; September 1991; 155(3): 263-268.

This article reports on a survey of California health care providers. While attitudes toward advance directives were positive, many physicians and nurses had little knowledge of advance directive options (even though their state had the earliest legislation on this matter) and were poorly equipped to discuss them with patients. The authors encourage staff education about advance health care planning, and also that provider concerns about the use of advance directives be addressed.

494. Haber, Joram G. The Living Will and the Directive to Provide Maximum Care: The Scope of Autonomy. Chest; September 1986; 90(3): 442-444.

The attorney author presents an ethical defense, based on the principle of self-determination, of the use of advance directives--either to limit or to demand medical interventions, depending on the patient's preferences--to aide in decision making for critically ill persons.

495. Henderson, Martha. Beyond the Living Will. Gerontologist; August

1990; 30(4): 480-485.

In a controlled study of residents of a retirement community, the author found that giving mentally capable individuals the opportunity to explicitly document their wishes in advance regarding future particular kinds of medical treatment, surrogate decisionmaking, and the like yielded important psychological benefits for those individuals. The appendix to the article gives an example of an addendum to a living will that allows for documentation of wishes regarding very specific treatments.

496. High, Dallas M. All in the Family: Extended Autonomy and Expectations in Surrogate Health Care Decision-Making. Gerontologist; June 1988; 28(Supplement): 46-51.

A philosopher interviewed a sample of elderly Kentucky residents about their desires and assumptions concerning advance directives and substitute medical decisionmaking in the event of subsequent incapacity. High found a substantial expectation and preference that families would naturally act as proxy decisionmakers, and an associated lack of concern about formal execution of advance directive documents.

497. Justin, Renate G. The Value History: A Necessary Family Document. Theoretical Medicine; 1987; 8: 275-282.

This article reports on the physician-author's experimentation with giving mentally capable patients the opportunity to fill out a questionnaire indicating their future medical treatment preferences and the values underlying those preferences. Patients responded positively to this opportunity to document their wishes. They also indicated that, in the absence of prior directives, they would want their families consulted about important decisions.

498. Kapp, Marshall B. Advance Health Care Planning: Taking a Medical Future. Southern Medical Journal; February 1988; 81(2): 221-224.

This article proposes, as a supplement to the currently available legal mechanisms for advance health care planning, namely the living will and durable power of attorney, that physicians begin regularly to use the "medical future." With this device, physicians would automatically, both at the time of initial contact and on a continuing basis, discuss with and collect data from their patients about future medical treatment preferences.

499. Kapp, Marshall B. Response to the Living Will Furor: Directives for Maximum Care. American Journal of Medicine; June 1982; 72(6): 855-859.

This article argues that a mentally capable person ought to be able to express future treatment preferences in favor of aggressive, life-prolonging medical intervention as well as for withholding or limiting such interventions. Allowing advance health care planning in either direction promotes patient autonomy, since many older persons fear both too much and too little medical attention.

500. Lambert, Pam; Gibson, Joan M.; Nathanson, Paul. The Values History: An Innovation in Surrogate Medical Decision-Making. Law, Medicine & Health Care; Fall 1990; 18(3): 202-212.

The authors present their proposed instrument for advance health care planning. This document would allow mentally capable adults to develop and express their personal fundamental ethical values concerning life, in a manner that could later be extrapolated to help health care providers and family members arrive at specific medical choices in the event of the patient's future incapacity. A copy of the instrument is included.

501. Lee, Melinda A.; Berry, Karen. Abuse of Durable Power of Attorney for Health Care: Case Report. Journal of the American Geriatrics Society; August 1991; 39(8): 806-809.

This article presents a case in which a relative of a decisionally incapacitated patient tried to use a Durable Power of Attorney to demand care which was in direct conflict with the patient's stated preferences and which, in the medical team's judgment, would be futile. This case illustrates ethical and practical problems that may arise regarding reliance on advance directives. These include improper execution of the directive, proxy decisions which are contrary to the prior wishes or present best interests of the patient, and conflicts of interest between the patient and proxy or others. Practical and procedural recommendations for resolving these tensions are set forth.

502. Lynn, Joanne. Why I Don't Have a Living Will. Law, Medicine & Health Care; Spring/Summer 1991; 19(1-2): 101-104.

A physician who is a prominent leader in the field of medical ethics explains why she has chosen consciously not to execute a formal advance directive. She believes that standard advance directive documents do not allow for the expression of sentiments about alternative futures that are important to care decisions near the end of life and that these documents do not give adequate respect to the expectation that the family and health care delivery system will do the "right" thing without being placed in a legal straightjacket. The author does not oppose the growth and development of advance directives, but wishes to expand the public and professional discussion of how to make decisions for incapacitated adults in order to include more varieties of formal and informal advance directives and to force policymakers to consider how to make decisions for incapacitated patients who have no advance directives.

503. Markson, Lawrence; Steel, Knight. Using Advance Directives in the Home-Care Setting. Generations; 1990; 14(Supplement): 25-28.

The authors offer observations on a pilot project using advance directives in a home care service. The project included an educational program for providers and was designed to allow physicians to help interested patients to complete durable powers of attorney. The authors conclude from their experience that it is possible for providers to routinely obtain and document preferences in advance of a medical crisis. The results of this project suggest that advance directives may be able to play an important role in enhancing personal autonomy in the home or institutional long term care setting.

504. McCrary, S. Van; Botkin, Jeffrey R. Hospital Policy on Advance Directives: Do Institutions Ask Patients About Living Wills? Journal of the American Medical Association; November 3, 1989; 262(17): 2411-2414.

A random survey found that, although almost half of American hospitals have an institutional ethics committee, these committees often are not involved in policy formulation for the institution regarding advance directives (living wills and durable powers of attorney). This article goes on to discuss ethical and legal issues concerning hospital policies on advance directives, arguing that a policy of asking patients about whether they have executed such a document is a matter of preventive ethics. The authors urge that ethics committees be permitted and even required to play a more active role in institutional policy development.

505. Miles, Steven H.; Gomez, Carlos F. Protocols for Elective Use of Life-Sustaining Treatments. New York: Springer Publishing Company; 1989.

This book is a design guide for health care institutions to use in developing and implementing formal policies and procedures regarding decision making regarding life-sustaining medical treatment. The authors elucidate the background of institutional protocols in this area, the process of protocol creation and adoption, and suggested protocol content.

506. Murphy, Donald J. Improving Advance Directives for Healthy Older People. Journal of the American Geriatrics Society; November 1990; 38(11): 1251-1256.

Dr. Murphy offers recommendations for improving both the quality and quantity of advance directives to limit life-sustaining medical treatment for older persons. Quality will improve when advance directives are written more specifically and those specific instructions are followed more literally. More people will execute advance directives when physicians spend more time discussing treatment and non-treatment options with patients prospectively. Physicians will be motivated to engage in such conversations by better Medicare reimbursement for this activity, although the role of education is also important.

507. National Conference of Commissioners on Uniform State Laws. Uniform Rights of the Terminally Ill Act. Chicago: NCCUSL; 1989.

This model piece of state legislation embodies and promotes the ethical principle of individual autonomy. The Act permits one to execute a declaration (living will) that instructs a physician to withhold or withdraw life-sustaining treatment in the event the person is terminally ill and decisionally incapacitated. In the alternative, the individual may execute a declaration (durable power of attorney) designating another person as her surrogate decisionmaker. The Act additionally authorizes a physician to withhold or withdraw life-sustaining treatment even in the absence of a declaration upon the consent of a close relative if the action would not conflict with the patient's known wishes.

508. New York State Task Force on Life and the Law. Life-Sustaining Treatment: Making Decisions and Appointing a Health Care Agent. New

York; July 1987.

The first half of this report extensively analyzes the ethical, social, and legal context for medical decision making, especially near the end of life. Applicable rights, responsibilities, and procedures for decision making by patients and their surrogates are discussed, as well as constraints on decision making. Special attention is focused on the ethical dilemmas of foregoing life-sustaining treatment--refusing intervention, decisions about artificial nutrition and hydration, and euthanasia. The second half of the report argues for enactment of a health care proxy law at the state level to help resolve some of the ethical dilemmas identified in the first half.

509. Raffin, Thomas A. Value of the Living Will. Chest; September 1986; 90(3): 444-446.

The author argues from a physician's perspective for the positive contribution of formal, as well as informal, advance directives in the process of choosing a course of care for the critically ill. He concludes that living wills may be extremely helpful to patients, families, and physicians in assisting them to deal with excruciatingly complex and emotionally wrenching medical decisionmaking dilemmas.

510. Rodriguez, Glenn S. Routine Discussion of Advance Health Care Directives: Are We Ready? An Opposing View. Journal of Family Practice; 1990; 31(6): 656-659.

The physician author encourages physicians to discuss future medical treatment preferences with their patients, and to respect and implement those preferences. However, Rodriguez suggests that such discussions be selective on the physician's part rather than routine.

511. Rosner, Fred. The Living Will. Chest; September 1986; 90(3): 441-442.

This editorial outlines some of the advantages and disadvantages of relying on advance directives for assistance in making difficult ethical issues concerning medical treatment for the critically ill.

512. Saultz, John. Routine Discussion of Advance Health Care Directives:

Are We Ready? An Affirmative View. Journal of Family Practice; 1990; 31(6): 653-656.

The physician author argues that primary care physicians ought to discuss future medical treatment preferences with their patients as an ordinary part of the course of medical care. Such timely discussions can reduce some of the ethical tension that arises where the wishes of a presently incompetent patient are unknown.

513. Schneiderman, Lawrence J.; Arras, John D. Counseling Patients to Counsel Physicians on Future Care in the Event of Patient Incompetence. Annals of Internal Medicine; May 1985; 102: 693-698.

The authors urge physicians to initiate and participate in conversations with their decisionally capable patients regarding future medical treatment decisions. Physicians should assist patients to document their preferences in the form of explicit, written advance proxy and instruction directives to assure respect for the patient's autonomous values and choices.

514. Zinberg, Joel M. Decisions for the Dying: An Empirical Study of Physicians' Responses to Advance Directives. Vermont Law Review; 1989; 13: 445-491.

In this study, the author interviewed physicians in Vermont and California regarding their experiences with and understanding of advance directives (i.e., living wills and durable powers of attorney). The results suggest that the availability of advance directives has had little effect on physicians' treatment of critically ill patients. The most important determinants of treatment decisions continue to be the traditional physician-patient-family consensus, the physician's perception--real or imagined--of potential civil or criminal liability, and the physician's moral treatment preferences. The author concludes that genuine self-determination for critically ill patients is unattainable.

515. Zweibel, Nancy; Cassel, Christine K. Treatment Choices at the End of Life: A Comparison of Decisions by Older Patients and Their Physician-Selected Proxies. Gerontologist; 1989; 29: 615-621.

This study utilized hypothetical vignettes describing scenarios in which decisions about the use of life-sustaining interventions are required for an older patient who cannot express autonomous preferences. When the responses of patients and their proxies are juxtaposed, some of the problems (e.g., differing perspectives on the older person's quality of life) inherent in relying on substitute decisionmakers to reflect patient treatment preferences become apparent. The study supports the importance of advance directives documenting treatment preferences.

10
Defining Death and Cadavers

516. Bernat, James L.; Culver, Charles M.; Gert, Bernard. Defining Death in Theory and Practice. Hastings Center Report; February 1982; 12(1): 5-9.

This article describes the ethical issues dealt with by the President's Commission for the Study of Ethical Problems in Medicine and Biomedical and Behavioral Research in its study and report on defining death. The authors criticize the Uniform Determination of Death Act (UDDA) that the Commission proposed as being too ambiguous.

517. Coller, Barry S. The Newly Dead As Research Subjects. Clinical Research; September 1989; 37(3): 487-494.

This article discusses the author's experience in conducting an experiment involving the use of newly dead persons as research subjects. Based on this experience and an analysis of relevant literature, Dr. Coller formulates ten ethical principles to guide researchers contemplating the use of new cadavers in their protocols.

518. Devettere, Raymond J. Neocortical Death and Human Death. Law, Medicine & Health Care; Spring/Summer 1990; 18(1-2): 96-104.

The author discusses proposals to make irreversible cessation of all neocortical or cerebral function a medical and legal indication of human death. Devetterre submits that neocortical cessation is consistent with our concepts of death and can, or soon will be, diagnosed in at least some cases with certainty, but that the concept is not and is not likely to be well understood by the general public. Thus, we should forsake efforts to establish it as a legal indication of death not because it is inappropriate or cannot be diagnosed, but because lack of public understanding will make this issue needlessly socially devisive.

519. Orlowski, James P.; Kanoti, George A.; Mehlman, Maxwell J. The Ethics of Using Newly Dead Patients for Teaching and Practicing Intubation Techniques. New England Journal of Medicine; August 18, 1988; 319(7): 439-441.

The justification for allowing physicians-in-training to learn intubation procedures by using newly dead patients must be assessed according to the need for such teaching, the claims of the interested parties, and relevant ethical and legal principles. In this essay, the authors conclude that the use of cadavers to teach intubation is justified but that, ideally, permission should be obtained by advance directive or from the next of kin.

520. President's Commission for the Study of Ethical Problems in Medicine and Biomedical and Behavioral Research. Defining Death: Medical, Legal and Ethical Issues in the Determination of Death. Washington, DC: U.S. Government Printing Office; July 1981.

This report examines the reasons for updating the societal definition of human death, discusses the medical state of the art in this area, probes the ethical and social meaning of alternative formulations (whole brain, higher brain, non-brain) of definitions of death, asks who properly ought to be redefining the concept of death, and suggests what definitions should be adopted ethically and legally.

521. Walker, A. Earl. Cerebral Death. Baltimore: Urban & Schwarzenberg; 1985.

This book examines, among other aspects of the subject, the ethical issues involved in the concept of brain death as compared with other ways that death might be defined.

11
Research With Older Human Subjects

522. Bell, J.A.; May, F.E.; Stewart, R.B. Clinical Research in the Elderly: Ethical and Methodological Considerations. Drug Intelligence and Clinical Pharmacy; 1987; 21: 1002-1007.

This article discusses some of the important ethical issues that arise with the use of older human subjects in biomedical research protocols.

523. Cassel, Christine. Ethical Issues in the Conduct of Research in Long Term Care. Gerontologist; June 1988; 28(Supplement): 90-96.

This meta-ethical study analyzed ethical issues identified in the conduct of research projects with older human subjects as part of the Retirement Research Foundation's Personal Autonomy in Long Term Care Initiative. Guidelines are presented concerning the proper setting and context of review for research in long term care, assessment of decisional capacity, and institutional strategies for reducing conflicts of interest.

524. Cassell, Christine K. Ethical Issues in Research in Geriatrics. Generations; Winter 1985; 10(2): 45-48.

This article discusses the 1978 Belmont Report of the National Commission for the Protection of Human Subjects of Biomedical and Behavioral Research. The three main ethical principles identified by the Commission were beneficence, respect for persons, and justice or equity. Dr. Cassell outlines these principles, with special reference to older human subjects.

525. Duffy, Linda M.; Wyble, S. J.; Wilson, B.; Miles, Steven H. Obtaining Geriatric Patient Consent. Journal of Gerontological Nursing; 1989; 15(1): 21-24.

This study of barriers to obtaining geriatric patient consent to research participation discusses the ethical bases for the consent requirement in the research context. The authors argue that, despite making research more difficult to carry out, consent must be respected ethically and neither overriden nor used as an excuse to exclude too quickly older patients who might personally benefit from participation in a research protocol.

526. Kaye, Janet M.; Lawton, Powell; Kaye, Donald. Attitudes of Elderly People About Clinical Research on Aging. Gerontologist; February 1990; 30(1): 100-106.

This study examined factors influencing the decisions of older persons regarding participation in biomedical and behavioral research. One characteristic of many subjects in the consenting group was a belief in the value of helping others through generation of new knowledge; this commitment to benefit others through one's actions may be described by the ethical principle of altruism.

527. Ratzan, Richard M. Being Old Makes You Different: The Ethics of Research With Elderly Subjects. Hastings Center Report; October 1980; 10(5): 32-42.

Dr. Ratzan discusses the special ethical considerations that arise when biomedical or behavioral research protocols propose to use older persons as research subjects. There is a need to take account of the older population's possible vulnerability in this context without becoming paternalistic. Ratzan suggests that valid consent to research participation by older persons should involve not only information, voluntariness, and decisional capacity, but also actual, accurate understanding of the experiment. The article presents an agenda for research on ethical problems in research.

528. Sachs, Greg A.; Cassel, Christine K. Biomedical Research Involving Older Human Subjects. Law, Medicine & Health Care; Fall 1990; 18(3): 234-243.

The physician authors comprehensively discuss ethical issues implicated by proposals to utilize cognitively impaired older persons as human subjects in biomedical and behavioral research protocols. The focus is on informed consent and the tension between the individual's autonomy and beneficence, especially in the long term care setting, while also considering societal interests.

529. Sachs, Greg A.; Rhymes, Jill; Cassel, Christine K. Letter, Research Ethics: Depression and Mortality in Nursing Homes.
Journal of the American Medical Association; July 10, 1991; 266(2): 215.

This letter comments on research that was conducted to determine the level of depression in nursing homes and its relationship to mortality. Issues are raised about the ethics of the researchers in not revealing a diagnosis of depression to the patient, family, or nursing home physician; keeping this diagnosis secret meant that the patient was deprived of treatment for depression unless it also was diagnosed independently. The authors additionally question whether meaningful informed consent was given for the researchers to keep to themselves diagnoses of depression.

530. Schwartz, Robert L. Informed Consent to Participation in Medical Research Employing Elderly Human Subjects. Journal of Contemporary Health Law and Policy; Spring 1985; 1(1): 115-131.

This article discusses the ethical, as well as the legal, problems that arise in the use of older persons as human subjects in biomedical and behavioral research protocols. Schwartz concentrates particularly on the use of demented individuals in research projects concerned with studying dementia.

531. Strain, Laurel A.; Chappell, Neena L. Problems and Strategies: Ethical Concerns in Survey Research with the Elderly. Gerontologist; December 1982; 22(6): 526-531.

This article describes ethical issues that arose in the conduct of several research projects of the authors that involved personal interviews with older persons. Ethical concerns are expressed regarding the subject's ability to give informed and voluntary consent for survey research participation, the obligations of the researcher to respond to problems or needs identified in the course of the interview, and demands for services made by the older person to the researcher for assistance.

532. Yordi, Cathleen L.; Chu, Amelia S.; Ross, Kathleen M.; Wong, Sylvia J. Research and the Frail Elderly: Ethical and Methodological Issues in Controlled Social Experiments. Gerontologist; February 1982; 22(1): 72-77.

The authors analyze the ethical problem that occurs in social science research protocols where members of vulnerable population groups, such as the frail elderly, may be denied potentially beneficial interventions because they have been assigned to the control or nonintervention group. The article describes an approach for managing sufficiently the control group participants' service needs without ruining the research design.

533. Zimmer, Anne; Calkins, Evan; Ostfeld, A.; Kaye, J.; Kaye, D. Conducting Clinical Research in Geriatric Populations. Annals of Internal Medicine; 1985; 103: 276-281.

Among other issues involved in biomedical research involving older human subjects, this paper discusses special ethical concerns. Particular attention is paid to questions concerning the use in research of persons with impaired cognitive abilities.

Author Index

References are to entry numbers, not to page numbers.

Subject Index

References are to entry numbers, not to page numbers.

About the Compiler

MARSHALL B. KAPP, J.D., M.P.H. is Professor in the Department of Community Health and Director of the Office of Geriatric Medicine & Gerontology, Wright State University School of Medicine and a member of the adjunct faculty at the University of Dayton School of Law, where he teaches a seminar on Law and Aging. His numerous books, journal articles, and presentations relate to ethical, legal, and public policy aspects of health care. He is the compiler of *Legal Aspects of Health Care for the Elderly: An Annotated Bibliography* (Greenwood Press, 1988).